M000311051

Vastarien

A Literary Journal

Issue Three

Jon Padgett, Editor-In-Chief

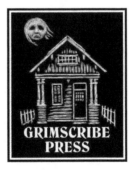

New Orleans, Louisiana

Published by
Grimscribe Press
New Orleans, LA
USA

https://vastarien-journal.com

CONTENTS

Acknowledgments   i

five dreams of the red tower   1
s. j. bagley

The Rules and Regulations of White Pines,   5
Vermont
Kurt Fawver

Long Time No See   19
F. J. Bergmann

Richard Gavin: The Nature of Horror   23
S. T. Joshi

The Mad German   45
Michael Uhall

I Feel Better Now   53
Brooke Warra

The Glow at Home   77
Rayna Waxhead

The Ghosts of Their Guns: Magical Realism in   89
the Fiction of Nadia Bulkin
S. L. Edwards

Chronology of a Burn   105
Tonya Liburd

The Blind Opera   117
Sean M. Thompson

Nightmares   135
Désirée Zamorano

"The Clown Puppet" — A Case Study   141
Michael Cisco

Nightly Senses   155
Emmie Bristow

The Nightmare Man   159
L'Erin Ogle

Ennigaldi   173
Sam Schreiber

Trauma Narrating   187
Dr. Raymond Thoss

For She is Falling   217
John Linwood Grant

Contributors   231

ACKNOWLEDGMENTS

Thanks to all the members of Thomas Ligotti Online and to our benefactors, including James Michael Baker, J. Black, Chris Cangiano, Iago Faustus, and Richard D. Hendricks.

five dreams of the red tower

By s. j. bagley

i dreamed of a street, cobblestone and crumbling, crooked as a jay's wing. i was walking, tripping over the stones, but never falling. i was wearing black leather shoes with heavy soles, ragged pants, no socks. at the end of the road, in the distance, was a tower, dark red in the afternoon sun. on either side of the street were empty storefronts, glassless and rotten, the occasional cat glaring from corners. at some point, the tower no closer no matter how much i've walked; a man in a freshly pressed black suit stepped in front of me, his hand against my chest. he began to speak in words i couldn't understand and i reached into my pocket, pulling out a small dull knife, which i proceeded to punch into his belly with a sound like the popping of some thick water balloon. he fell to his knees and i stood above him, casting my knife to the side, grabbing his hair and pulling back. with his mouth open to me, my whole body began to heave and shudder until i forcefully vomited an impossible amount of ticks, dry and scrambling, which crawled into his mouth and down his gullet. once i was spent and there were no more of them, he stood, reached his hand within the wound in his belly, and pulled out a small jack in the box: rusty, yellow and red. i put it in my pocket and continued walking towards the tower as he walked in the direction i had come.

(two.)

i dreamed of a child's room, decorated in a fashion from decades past, walls covered in peeling strips of cowboys and dinosaurs; the surface underneath black with mold, dry and dusty. on the ruin of a bed was a small package covered in stamps and stickers, as if it had been on a journey around the world before arriving in this sad little room. i picked it up, brown paper wrapper crumbling beneath the damp twine that held it. i stood with it in my hands for a while before untying the twine, casting it onto the bed, and peeling back the paper. inside was a toy clown head, cold tin and warm rubber, its eyes glass marbles, cat's eyes moving with the motion of my breath. i held it up and saw that there was a small turnkey on the back. i turned it four times and let go and it made a shrieking metallic laugh, like a dying man— or a hyena. it grew warm and sick as it laughed and i threw it to the corner of the room, wiping my hands upon my pants and i picked up the wrapper, again. the only words i could make out from the sender's address was the word: 'tower.' the air in the room grew cold and smelled of meat, long since turned.

(three.)

i dreamed of being in a small cell, steel bars black with age, concrete floor worn smooth. i was barefoot, only wearing rough trousers. in the cells around me, i could hear heavy breathing as if, somehow, inside some massive sleeping beast. after some time, a man, thin and tall, came to the door with an envelope. i could not make out his features, as he slid the envelope between the bars and then ran off. i crawled across the floor, unable to move my legs, and grabbed the crisp paper, tearing it open; small plastic silver stars pouring out to the cold floor, as i pulled out the single small piece of pink paper. an invitation to some garden party, addressed to someone else, the location listed as 'somewhere you know the way to.' and, somehow, i did.

(four.)

i dreamed of being at a table in the corner of a quiet restaurant, lit by candles. across the table was a man i could barely make out, the light of the candles reflected in his glasses and his greasy beard. we spoke of distant lands and he told me that he left part of his stomach beneath a tower, bits of it entwined in the springs of some horrible novelty toy. i asked if he was in pain. he wetly chuckled and began to describe the room he left part of his stomach in. i grew cold with fear, anxiety causing my teeth to chatter. i blew out the candles on our table so i could no longer see him.

(five.)

i dreamed of walking through a room filled with boxes of marbles and old toys, bent and broken, each one seeming wrong, somehow. i picked up a bit of flattened tin with a clown's face painted on it and metal clackers attached to the front and back. i wiggled it quickly, causing the clackers to clack against it, much too loud for the space i was in. i kept playing with the noisemaker, weeping, knowing i would soon be finished.

Credit: Aeron Alfrey

The Rules and Regulations of White Pines, Vermont

By Kurt Fawver

Rules and Regulations of White Pines, Vermont
Written and made available by the White Pines Community Council

Introduction:

You've decided to settle in beautiful White Pines! Wonderful! You're about to become one of the over three-hundred residents of a town that is, without exaggeration, a tiny piece of heaven on earth.

For almost two centuries, White Pines has stood as a testament to a simpler and better way of life. Here in White Pines, we believe in charity, love, and dedication to our neighbors—virtues that have made us a largely self-sufficient and self-sustaining community. If you don't want to travel dozens of miles to a grocery store or your child's school or your demoralizing job, well, don't worry, because you won't have to! We have a foolproof system that will take care of all those headaches and allow you to live as the divine spirit of creation intended!

Given that many of our residents have been raised in the urban and suburban blight to the south, you might be naturally concerned about crime, but in White Pines the crime rate has remained stable at absolute zero for many, many decades. You don't even need to lock your door at night! And if you're worried about your health? Well, the very air in White Pines must be an elixir of life, since, at 99.9 years, the median lifespan of a White Pinesian is over twenty years longer than the national average! We grow 'em good and ripe up here in the mountains! Despite not holding "traditional" jobs (though we think the jobs in our town are actually the most traditional of all), you'll also find White Pines residents are never in want of money, goods, or services. We make sure your needs are met so you can explore what it truly means to be a human BEING rather than a human DOING.

So, what, you might have already asked yourself, is the catch? Truly, there isn't one. We've met you, interviewed you, and you've been welcomed to join us! If you can simply adhere to a few basic rules and regulations that all White Pinesians abide by, you'll be set! Trust us, they're easy to understand and even easier to follow. In no time at all, you won't even think of them as rules, but as your natural way of living!

Without further ado, then, here are…

The Rules and Regulations of White Pines:

1. **You must love history and be glad to celebrate it.** White Pines has a long and storied past, and we cherish that fact. Especially important to us, and commemorated with a Pioneer Festival each year, is our founding by Henry Ember and Thomas Childs, two scholars from early nineteenth century Boston. Ember, a schoolteacher, and Childs, a minor poet, had been heavily influenced by the Transcendentalist movement sweeping the young nation. Both believed a return to the wilderness would bring humankind back into alignment with its inherent perfection and both believed it was their duty to aid in this process. They saw themselves as ministers of a humanist-naturalist faith, gentle heroes who might flush the poisons of the world from the body politic. With the most noble of intentions, Ember and Childs set out, like many other visionaries of their day, to build a sylvan utopia. Over the course of several years, they recruited skilled workers to join their community and, in 1839, once their numbers had grown to just over sixty men and women, they trekked northwest in search of a rural idyll in which to plant the seeds of a new Eden. White Pines is the fruit that grew from that labor. We believe it only right to remember and give thanks for such forward thinking and bravery, without which we would not know the paradise that is our town.

2. **You must love nature and seek to conserve it.** Our community is hemmed in on all sides by the breathtaking Green Mountains, and our founders intended it to be so. They wanted to inhabit a land so remote that the power and majesty of nature would be unavoidable and all-pervasive. By inundating their senses with the natural world, they hoped to create psychic barriers between White Pines and the corrupt civilization they'd left behind. They were sure that a moss-lined glade

was better than a soot-belching factory, that a field of flowers was better than a field of dead soldiers, that the bite from a rattlesnake was better than the bite from a mugger's knife. Turns out, they were right! You'll see that nature is central to our way of life. From our buildings—every last one a log cabin—to our food—all of which is resourced directly from the mountains around us, nature provides for us an unimaginable bounty. In White Pines, we have never experienced drought or flood, famine or blight. We have never gone without a meal nor have we ever wanted for shelter or heat or even a cool breeze on a summer's day. We've remained untouched by diseases and illnesses that decimate other places, other peoples. Nature delivers all this to us and, in return, only asks that we give respect and a bit of sacrifice. It's more than a fair trade-off, we're sure you'll agree.

3. **You must visit Ember's Hole and listen to your name echo in its depths.** There is no feature of the surrounding wilderness so important to our town as Ember's Hole. In fact, Henry Ember and Thomas Childs chose the location of White Pines based solely on its proximity to the hole. From the outset, they recognized the hole's significance as a unique natural feature that could be found nowhere else in New England or, very possibly, the entire world. When you visit the hole, you'll immediately notice exactly what Ember, Childs, and their band of dreamers did—that within fifty paces of the vast depression, sound does not carry. You'll speak but hear nothing; birds above will chirrup and tweet, but their songs will not reach you; even the wind itself cannot whistle in your ear. As you move closer to the hole, you'll become acquainted with its shape and dimensions: a perfect circle with a diameter of nine feet, nine inches. If you hover by the edge of this circle, you'll begin to hear noises from deep within its lightless recesses.

credit: Yves Tourigny

The sounds that the surrounding area lacks will seem to you collected, compressed, and distorted far, far below the earth's crust. It is not unusual to hear what you may believe to be pleas or lamentations issue from the hole. Trust that these are mere distortions of the noises of the natural world and no more. From your position on the precipice, then, you will kneel and hang your head over the abyss. Many newcomers stare into the hole and wonder what lies at its terminus. Many feel a sensation they've never felt before, a perfect serenity and stillness at the center of a cyclone of fear—Henry Ember and Thomas Childs called it the "dread peace." All this is to be expected. No matter what happens to you, whether your experiences at the hole are usual or unusual, you must speak your name into the darkness and wait for it to be repeated to you. Once you hear your voice swirling through the rushes of the harrowing ambience, you will begin to understand what it means to be a part of White Pines.

4. You must care for your White Pines neighbors and treat them as brothers and sisters. A rumor you'll hear about town is that Norman Rockwell stumbled upon White Pines as a young man and based many of his illustrations and paintings on scenes he witnessed while in our community. While we can neither confirm nor deny the veracity of that rumor, we can say that the bucolic harmony in many of Rockwell's works is exactly what you'll experience in White Pines. It's rare to see a frowning face about town, and it's rarer to hear a heated argument. You'll never be caught up in a drunken brawl—though we do imbibe frequently—and you'll never be cheated out of your fair share of our goods. Some of us claim that even babies don't cry within our borders. There's a humming spirit of togetherness that you can't help but let reverberate inside you. It draws out frustration and anger and sadness and replaces them with a universe of contented smiles. Open yourself to this spirit, this vibrato of perfect community, and we're certain you'll come to love each and every member of the White Pines family.

5. You must take time to reflect on the joys of living in White Pines and the luck you had in finding us. We don't ask for reverence or worship, but we do implore you to contemplate the happiness our town will inevitably cultivate within you. Think on the fact that your pantry is always stocked with fine, organic meats and cheeses and grains and vegetables, even when you don't restock it yourself and that the generator that powers your cabin is always filled with gasoline. Think on the miracle of your children learning to read and write and manipulate numbers without ever listening to a teacher's drone or setting themselves to a page of homework. Think on the impossibility that whatever material goods you request from the town council, they will provide to you regardless of cost. Think on the revelation that your life consists of simply being, that you can choose to sit on your porch and stare at clouds practically all day, every day, and no one will force you to do otherwise. And always remember that exceedingly few people manage to discover our town. You are one of a rarified group selected by happenstance or destiny or the hand of a higher power to stumble upon us. Whether you lost your way from a hiking trail or a camping trip or a Bigfoot hunting expedition, your path through the wilderness led you here—a statistical improbability, considering the acreage of the Green Mountain range. You should have run into a road or a stream and followed its rush back to the corruption of civilization. You should have died from hypothermia, from dehydration, from falling off a rock face or worse. You should have never been able to find us. Yet here you are in White Pines. Consider that tremendous improbability and know you won a cosmic contest you didn't even have to enter.

6. You must participate in the lunar drawing and select a named location from your chosen coordinates if you win the drawing. Twice per month—once on the evening of the full moon and again on the evening of the new moon—we hold a lottery in the center of town. During the lottery, everyone in the community gathers around a hollow wooden globe carved by one of White Pines' founding members during the mid-nineteenth century. Cut into the north pole of the globe is a hole and from that hole a member of the town council randomly pulls a slip of paper with the name of a White Pines resident written upon it. The globe is then emptied and refilled with new slips of paper. If you're the White Pinesian whose name was selected, you will draw out six of these new pieces of paper—all of which will be inscribed with a letter N, S, E, or W and numerals ranging from zero to one hundred and eighty. These six numbers form latitudinal and longitudinal coordinates that you, the lottery winner, must subsequently plot on a detailed world map held in possession by the town council. You will then list the nine nearest human settlements to the intersection of the coordinates—be they thriving cities or nameless villages—and choose one of these settlements for a special honor. How you select the settlement is entirely at your discretion. Some White Pinesians like to close their eyes and point to one; others simply pick the name that nestles most comfortably in their ears. No matter how you choose, you will eventually close upon one place, one habitation, and inform the town council of your decision, after which you may resume your normal activities and routines and forget all about the lottery.

7. **You must perform a service for White Pines and be glad to give back to the town.** At random intervals, certain jobs become unavoidable. However, the work we undertake in our community is unlike work in the wider world. At a necessary and proper time, the town council will seek you out and ask for your assistance in dealing with a problem. You cannot refuse to help. Often, the task set before you will be opaque. You might have to walk to a nearby dirt road, find an abandoned car, and drive it to a second location; you might have to venture into the forests and pick specified berries and mushrooms, which you'll be asked to crush into a paste; you might have to carry an unmarked package to a mailbox in a wayward hamlet and make sure it's picked up for delivery; you might have to dig a ditch deep in the forest and sprinkle lye flakes across its bottom. It's impossible to speculate what service the council may ultimately need you to perform. Though you may not understand the need for a particular labor, rest assured that each and every action builds toward the maintenance of White Pines and its way of life. It's only through these small gestures of solidarity and allegiance that we manage to remain a safe haven removed from the degradation of civilization and its harmful, ever-extending grasp.

8. You must let go of the world beyond our borders and distrust its encroachment. Although we have satellite television and internet thanks to one of our technologically savvy residents, you'll find we rarely speak of the world outside White Pines. It's not that we don't track its progress or borrow from its advances, but that its general existence threatens ours. When Henry Ember and Thomas Childs shrugged off Boston, they shrugged off the yolk of responsibility to the teeming masses of the city. They understood that not everyone can or should be a member of White Pines. For White Pines to function in its current pristine state, it must remain separate and self-contained. It must remain a space apart. Our peace and prosperity are built upon adherence to our specific rules and regulations, but not all people would respect, let alone follow, those rules. Just imagine if everyone and anyone tried to move here! Our natural splendor would be slashed away, our sense of community would be stretched paper thin, and our traditions would be diluted or supplanted. All the benefits of living in White Pines, all the privileges, all the uniqueness, would crumble. You see then why, for the sake of our town and your own happiness, you must begin to conceive of the world outside our town as a lost cause. Paradise can ill afford an open-door policy.

9. You must agree to be lowered into Ember's Hole and etch a name on its walls. Following lunar drawings, the town council will instruct one member of our community to spelunk into Ember's Hole and etch the name of the lottery winner's chosen settlement into the hole's rock face. Henry Ember was the first to do so and, when it comes your time, you will follow suit. Upon discovering the hole, Ember and Childs experienced what they referred to as "a revelation of the roots of the world in their widest extensions." They wrote that "the hole is where these roots call out for nourishment and where we must supply them

13

such, if they are to bear our community as their brightest and fullest bloom." Thus, we have fertilized those roots twice per month, every month, since our founding. Inside the hole, under the tides of rebounding sound, you will find hundreds of names carved into the rock face. Bhopal. Halifax. Aberfan. Dhaka. Benxi. Texas City. Oppau. Some of these names may be familiar to you. Most will be entirely foreign. Ignore them all. You have one reason for entering the hole and one reason alone: to strike a new name into the lightless places. During this process, you'll be suspended by a secure harness inside a cavity that, to the present day, has never been able to be measured to its floor. A crisp odor some have likened to blood will drift into your nostrils and mouth. Your sole source of illumination will be a pocket flashlight. You will be battered by potentially disturbing noises which are often reported to increase in number and volume when you begin etching a new place into the hole. Given these conditions, you will not have the resources—physically or psychologically—to take account of the individual locales listed along the long, downward spiral. Therefore, it is best to simply chisel the name given to you into an open space upon the wall and signal for your return. After you've been pulled back to the surface and are free of the duty, we're sure you'll agree that spending more time inside Ember's Hole collecting names is the last thing you or any White Pinesian wants to do. Instead, return to your long life of peace and leisure and enjoy the reward that feeding Ember's "roots" affords you.

10. **You must keep the knowledge of White Pines to yourself and help maintain its secrecy.** Since we've established that White Pines requires strict separation from the greater world if it's to bestow its benefits to its members, the next logical step is to safeguard that separation. The wonders of our community are manifold, but they are

fragile. Even a single misspoken word to a relative or acquaintance who doesn't live in White Pines could open our town to infection. This means that you cannot invite family to visit; you cannot tell friends where you live; you cannot list White Pines as an address on any document, anywhere. Though we do not require it, we strongly suggest that you rely on your fellow White Pinesians for love and friendship and find the strength to cut yourself off from those who still reside in the outside world. We know this is difficult but doing so will alleviate the temptation to divulge information of White Pines' existence and whereabouts. If at any point in your infrequent travels beyond our borders you do hear non-residents talking about White Pines, you must prevent such persons from continuing their dialogues. Preferred methods of prevention include derision, distraction, and drowning out the speakers. Other, more extreme methods of prevention are available and will be outlined by the town council in an individual meeting with you once you've become a long-term resident. Although occasionally necessary, we suggest utilizing these alternative, more extreme silencing methods sparingly, as they often draw unwanted attention too near our community. Perfection, we've found, flowers best in shadow.

11. **You must value tradition and honor its fundamental place in our community's existence.** White Pines stands upon a solid bedrock of stasis. As with any endeavor that accomplishes its goals, we see little reason to promote change when our system of living works better than any other in all the history books in all the world. For nearly two hundred years, we have maintained a quality of life that grants extreme longevity, unparalleled security, and total material prosperity. Our traditions serve as the pillars that prop up and stabilize such a life. Some of these key customs we've outlined in this document—the lottery, the etching of names, and the performance of council tasks for example.

Others, like the annual spring warding or the recitation of Thomas Childs' "Ode to the Rift" before town meetings, you will come to know through your basic citizenly participation in White Pines. No matter how you encounter our traditions, you must respect them and understand that they are necessary threads in the protective tapestry that enfolds us. If you tug at one too hard, it may unravel and undermine the integrity of the entire fabric. But if you safeguard each and every fiber, the cloth may last forever.

12. **You must refrain from thinking about the names etched on the walls of Ember's Hole and the jobs you perform for the town council.** Wondering at the meaning of the names and the purpose of the tasks will set you on a path to paranoia and anxiety. While occasional conjecture among other White Pinesians concerning these topics is expected and perhaps even healthy, we insist that exploration into these issues be limited to the realm of the abstract. A lively philosophical discussion about the power of names or the value of isolation or even the nature of production and scarcity would be encouraged. An investigative project that attempts to specifically link these concepts with Ember's Hole and White Pines' practices, however, while not explicitly prohibited, would be discouraged in the strongest terms. Past instances of community members embarking upon such projects has resulted in expulsion, re-education, and other, less congenial forms of censure. If your curiosity concerning the basis for our various ceremonies and functions simply cannot be contained, perhaps you will need to turn your inquisitive mind upon yourself. Why do you need to know how words like "Nakhon" and "Pathom" relate to the full set of rare action figures that appear in your cabin when your child asks for them? How does it enrich your life to note that the packages you've been tasked with mailing are, by and large, addressed

to journalists? What good can come of recording the cacophony that emanates from Ember's Hole and singling out individual voices that wail for lost children and lovers and parents and friends? How can your life, a life lived in near-total comfort and ease, be made better through any of the knowledge you seek? Answer questions such as these first, before you continue your explorations into the deep state of White Pines. Through your self-examination, we believe that you will realize any true heaven requires a margin of blissful ignorance. Of course, if you fail to reach this conclusion, we hold no liability for your future wellbeing.

13. **You must agree that the perfection of White Pines is sacrosanct and adhere to the rules that safeguard its existence.** Although we cherish each and every member of our community, the overarching project of White Pines is far more important than any individual. Henry Ember and Thomas Childs set out to expand what it could mean to be a fully realized human being, free from the chains of want, free from the poisons of civilization, and free from the blades of hatred that cut deep in every other corner of the world. White Pines is the attainment of those dreams. Uphold the rules set forth in this document and you'll contribute to a genuine utopia. Disregard or break the rules and, as a cowed Adam and Eve discovered before you, you'll be subject to harsh penalties. We're certain you'll make the right decisions and act as an upstanding citizen of our community. Welcome home.

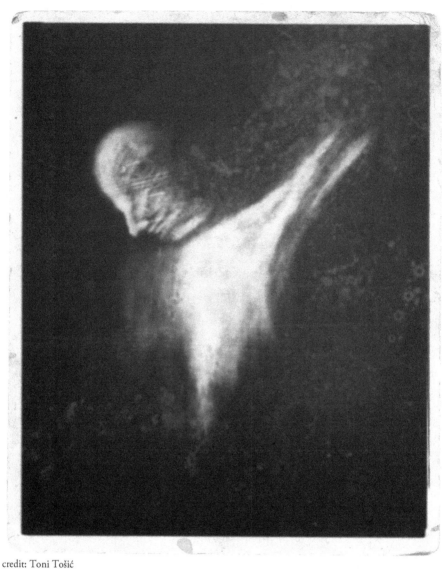

credit: Toni Tošić

Long Time No See

By F. J. Bergmann

It has been quite a long time
since I have seen my mother,
but, after all, for many months
before she died I made a point
of not visiting except to pick up
her granddaughters, who agreed
to make the best of a difficult
situation (carping, obstruction,
grudges). When she was still
walking, the best she could do
was a hundred feet per hour;
she would often stop, turn

around and around, and glare
at the sidewalk. On a lucky day,
maybe someone might take pity
on her, invite her in (a decision
they would regret). Her ashes
were scattered in the location
selected long before her death,
but she had never gone there
on foot. The short (they tell me)
ceremony took place during
a windy day, on a grassy hill.
Reassembling her molecules
(and her essence, of course—
that mélange of suspicion,
preening, and status-seeking)
from wherever they had been
transported must have posed
quite a challenge, but she throve
on adversity—to say nothing of
thwarting others. I can imagine
that she found it easier to return
to her home first and then strike
north again than to traverse
a direct route to mine. Still, even
allowing for vagaries of terrain
and the need to travel during
hours of darkness, away from
traffic, the intervening years
are drawing to an end; I expect

that some night soon I will find her
her standing on the threshold,
waiting for me to open the door.

Richard Gavin: The Nature of Horror

By S. T. Joshi

F OR MORE than a decade, Canadian writer Richard Gavin (b. 1974) has been quietly amassing an enviable reputation as an author of weird tales that fuse sensitivity to the strangeness inherent in landscape with a keen insight into human emotions, expressed in prose that provides its own sensuous pleasures all apart from the subject matter. He is the author of five short story collections: *Charnel Wine* (2004), *Omens* (2007), *The Darkly Splendid Realm* (2009), *At Fear's Altar* (2012), and *Sylvan Dread* (2016). Gavin has also written a volume of "esotericism," *The Benighted Path: Primeval Gnosis and the Monstrous Soul* (2015), and co-edited an anthology of occult fiction, *Penumbrae* (2015). Each of his story collections exhibits an incremental improvement over its predecessor, and each of them features capable and occasionally brilliant and powerful weird tales that hark back to the legacy of Arthur Machen, Algernon Blackwood, H. P. Lovecraft, and other classic writers.

Gavin's interest in the occult is genuine and affects his understanding of weird fiction in a direct way. In a prologue to the tale (or vignette) "Fragments of a Primordial Gnosis" (in *Charnel Wine*), he writes:

> It has long been a belief of mine that horror is a direct link to primordial consciousness. I am of the opinion that certain strands of the macabre tale, when well-crafted, can pry open doorways in the psyche that would have otherwise remained sealed, thus prohibiting a vast panorama of profound personal experiences. In order to facilitate this "prying open" process, I attempt to write fiction that is as close to its transcendental (or perhaps infernal) source as possible.[1]

It is not entirely how seriously Gavin wishes us to take this utterance, for the prologue is meant to introduce the series of "fragments" that Gavin claims to have received from an unknown British correspondent. This prologue is apparently a fictional construct that is designed to set the stage for the rather nebulous sketch that follows. But Gavin has written a foreword to *Omens* that addresses the issue somewhat less ambiguously. Here he focuses on the nightmare, which he maintains is "a fleeting glimpse into a rich and vital dimension of consciousness".[2] While recognising that not all nightmares "are the by-products of the universe trying to pass on some

---

[1] Richard Gavin, *Charnel Wine* (Colusa: Dark Regions Press, 2004), 35.
[2] Ibid., xi.

form of teaching,"[3] a certain number of them are, or may be. Gavin then makes an explicit connection with weird fiction:

> This veiled glimpsing of vast truths connects the nightmare with the horror story.
>
> One of the great trade secrets of macabre literature is that in any effective tale, the supernatural element (or elements) must always be larger than their appearance within the tale itself. An author may introduce vast supernatural forces into a plotline, but the author may never (and, in all likelihood, *can* never) fully explain these forces. For example, a writer can craft a thoroughly chilling and convincing haunted house story without having to resort to an in-depth analysis of how hauntings occur. The reader can relish the *effects* of a haunting even when the author decides to forego a pseudoscientific explanation at the tale's conclusion.[4]

Gavin also notes that the "technique of vagueness" can be put to good use in the weird tale, since "the strength of this kind of horror story lies in the fact that its reality is akin to nightmare reality."[5] This shows Gavin drifting in the direction of the ambiguity of Robert Aickman, and indeed some of his later tales betray a decided influence from that author.

Charnel Wine is a somewhat rudimentary volume, full of tales that show promise but also flaws in conception and execution, as well as brief sketches or prose-poems whose insubstantiality make analysis

---

[3] Ibid.
[4] Ibid., xii-xiii.
[5] Ibid., xiii.

difficult. In accordance with Gavin's stated principles of weird writing, a number of the tales feature a succession of events whose logic and coherence are not easily deducible by the reader, but that nonetheless generate a clutching atmosphere of terror. The title story is one of the more easily understandable narratives—and one of the best. Here a woman, Jessica, tells how her partner, Finnegan, has horrible nightmares of corpses. She casts an incantation to make him sleep. As the story proceeds, we learn that Jessica has in fact revived Finnegan from the dead. As she ruefully remarks, "Death, it seems, is far more adept than I at snatching souls."[6]

Other tales do not quite deliver on their grandiose premises. "Reflections from the Abyss" takes us to a house designed by an eccentric architect—a house that contains strange creatures the architect denotes simply as *"They"*:

> Translucent shapes hovered against the cold darkness of the mirrored walls. . . . The shapes hovered behind the mirrored glass like exotic fish in an aquarium. The creatures, vaguely sperm-like in appearance, squirmed within churning funnels of clear light. The apparitions seemed horribly delicate. The spiralling vortexes seemed to emanate from a darkness more primordial than the mere absence of light.[7]

The influence of Lovecraft's "From Beyond" (1920) may be seen here, as that tale similarly tells of a scientist who designs a machine that allows for the perception of transparent creatures floating in the air all around us. But Gavin's story, interesting as its conception is,

---

[6] Ibid., 13.
[7] Ibid., 21.

seems to be developed somewhat crudely.

"The Lodge" begins as a moving tale of teenage love and friendship, whereby a boy named Peter leads his friends to a remote building called the Lodge into which he maintains his father had disappeared, and now *"we're going in there to find him."*[8] But vagueness and clumsy development mar this promising beginning. "The Folly" similarly promises too much, speaking of the doom of all humanity without clarifying how the disturbing but relatively mundane events of the story could bring about that result.

But *Charnel Wine* contains more than its share of successes, including "Parting the Veils," an account of a despondent man (he is recently divorced) stumbling into a warehouse that contains dead bodies. When one of the bodies—that of a young woman—suddenly reaches out to seize his arm, a friend appears and states that the woman is "not quite brained yet, but I should have her ready to escort you to my next soirée."[9] There is a fine atmosphere of dreamlike fantasy here. "Porcelain and Pretty Lace" is narrated by an eleven-year-old girl whose younger sister has died—and whom a dollmaker has somehow managed to turn into a living doll. Will the surviving sister be next?

"The Physics of Unseen Puppeteers," dedicated to Thomas Ligotti, utilizes Ligotti's patented theme of the puppet or marionette to suggest the notion that all human beings are puppets, manipulated by some nameless cosmic entity. Another story that is far more than a pastiche is "Berenice's Journal," an homage to—and perhaps a parody of—Poe's story of a man fixated by a woman's teeth. "Feet of Clay, Head of Fire" is an engaging story about the German weird writer,

---

[8] Ibid., 47.
[9] Ibid., 75.

Gustav Meyrink.

Charnel Wine contains a trilogy of tales about an enigmatic physician, Dr. Otto Valzer. The first, "Flowers of Delirium," is a grim and compelling tale of homunculi—in this case, a tiny human skeleton found in the skull of people who died of rheumatic fever. Valzer himself seems afflicted with such an entity when he falls ill; and when he dies, a hundred such creatures are released. An alternate version of Valzer's death is supplied in "The Master's Posthumous Sermon," although this tale is a bit meandering. Finally, "Leavings of Shroud House: An Inventory" has Valzer on television narrating the various curious objects found in the house of the title, a "veritable museum of occult materials."[10] There is no particular unity to the story, even though the first-person narrator maintains that the objects might somehow "unravel the mystery of the endless haunting of the human race,"[11] but the individual episodes are effective.

Omens is a slim collection, but one that features more full-fledged stories rather than the sketches, vignettes, and prose-poems that filled *Charnel Wine.* Here too are a certain number of less-than-successful tales, such as "The Pale Lover," an unsatisfactory mix of sex and occultism; "Down among the Relics," a confused story about a man who may have witnessed an elderly man killing several of his classmates; "Strange Advances," a rambling and unfocused tale that seeks to capture the ambiguity of Aickman (the story is dedicated to him) but ends up being merely confusing; and a similarly meandering tale, "What Blooms in Shadow Withers in Light," which purports to highlight the terror inherent in Halloween.

---

[10] Ibid., 123.
[11] Ibid., 133.

But *Omens* should be judged by its successes, not its failures. "A For[12]m of Hospice" is a prototypical example of Gavin's fascination with dreams and nightmares. The narrator, afflicted with cancer, seeks help from an unorthodox practitioner called Benjamin Keep, who specializes in "dreams and sleep." The narrator himself has long had vivid dreams, so perhaps Keep can help him. But he later realises that Keep "was not providing the sick with an entry into an astral paradise; he was using them to provide entry for the twisted things that no longer wished to be confined to the realm of dark dreams."[13] The slow but sure pacing of the tale, and its gradual revelation of the cataclysmic denouement, admirably display Gavin's grasp of short story technique.

"The Bellman's Way" is a haunting tale of rural horror. The painter Clayton Grant moves into a rural chapel that has been turned into a residence; he settles there with his wife, Laura, and nine-year-old daughter, Julia. When, one night, he sees the odd figure of a bellman walking by his house, he is told by the local constable: "He wards away the far-off things, the things that don't belong here."[14] That ominous statement makes Clayton wonder whether he and his family might be one of those things; and in a thrilling climax, he pursues the bellman, who is perhaps making away with his daughter. The tale ends somewhat obscurely, but its atmosphere of nebulous terror is unmatched.

"Daniel" begins strikingly with a man holding in his hand his wife's severed head. But only much later do we understand that it was his small son, Daniel, who killed his own mother. Both father and son

---

[12] Richard Gavin, *Omens* (Poplar Bluff: Mythos Books, 2007), 104.
[13] Ibid., 109.
[14] Ibid., 35.

are afflicted with what the father calls Hellbrain:

> Hellbrain feels exactly as you think it would: chaotic and agonizing. It starts with a dizzy feeling, like something living is convulsing at the base of your skull. . . . Then comes the burning; a fiery pain that I don't have the words to describe to you. It *sears* you. It burns so deeply you can actually see the glow, like fresh-cut rubies, like embers, like sin.
>
> Hellbrain makes the world turn poppy-flower red. Everything you see, every thought that wisps through your mind, scorches you.
>
> And there's a buzzing in your ears, like a chorus of cicadas shrilling within the cave of your skull.[15]

The strangely titled "& on the Eve of Yule . . ." is a bizarre vignette about a boy who finds an incredibly aged man confined in a trunk in his aunt's house. There is some fine horrific imagery in the tale, but its overall symbolism remains a trifle opaque.

With *The Darkly Splendid Realm* and, especially, *At Fear's Altar*, Gavin attains the pinnacle of his achievement thus far in the short story. In the former, we have such gems as "Dreaming While Adrift on the River of Despair," a strangely poignant vignette about a woman who doesn't know that she has been resurrected from the dead by her lover, who happens to be a mortician (the story is thematically similar to "Charnel Wine," but superior to that tale), and "The Language of the Nameless Region," an atmospheric account of man (curiously named Om) who lures a woman to her death by giving her a scarf

---

[15] Ibid., 54.

made of spiderwebs—an object that may be one of the "dream relics"[16] he has collected.

The volume contains several tales that probe deeply into domestic and familial conflict by means of the supernatural. Consider "Getting the Strap." Here a boy whose parents are dead is raised by his grandmother, who beats him regularly with a leather strap. During his college years, he is forced to place her in a nursing home, where she dies nine years later. When the man marries, he engages in an affair; guilt-ridden, he wants his lover to beat him with a leather belt. What has up to this point been a grim story of the lasting legacy of abuse turns supernatural when, after the lover flees, the ghost of the grandmother emerges and takes up the belt to inflict the punishment the man desires.

"Prowling through Throated Chambers" is a tale that uses a man's fascination with waxworks to underscore his tortured relations with his father. The man is a photographer and envisions a book about "all the waxworks Chambers of Horrors and sideshow spook houses I could find."[17] When a roommate tells him that there is such a place nearby that was "so frightening it had actually been condemned by the Board of Health,"[18] the man cannot resist exploring it. The twists and turns of the narrative become numerous at this point, but the end result is a chilling exhibition of a family torn apart by crime and guilt.

"Waterburns" is a richly complex tale of two sisters, Nancy and Agatha, and the different ways they dealt with a horrible burned figure who emerges from a lake when they were children. Nancy, failing to recover from the trauma, kills herself at seventeen. Agatha bears a

---

[16] Richard Gavin, *The Darkly Splendid Realm* (Colusa: Dark Regions Press, 2009), 114.

[17] Ibid., 16.

[18] Ibid., 17.

child at sixteen, but when the boy turns sixteen he dies in a car accident: he is, in fact, the burned figure that the girls saw. Later Agatha walks into the lake, presumably to drown herself, but she emerges at the farther shore: her appearance terrifies two small boys. In this way Gavin suggests that the cycle of horror is ongoing.

"The Bitter Taste of Dread-Moths" is a long and somewhat meandering story of a woman who, at the age of nine, suffered a traumatic event (she found a dying baby in an abandoned office building). Gavin once again resurrects the figure of Dr. Valzer, who has written a book about the Ku-Leng cult and its notions that fear can become embodied in a Dread-Moth. There are so many interesting elements in this story that are insufficiently realized that Gavin would be well advised to consider turning it into a novel.

Then there is the novelette "Primeval Wood," which opens with a luminous paragraph that demonstrates Gavin's mastery of evocative prose:

> Certain miracles are reserved for the wayward and the damned. For just as every paradise has its netherworld and each metropolis its slum, the miraculous has its averse kin. Most people pass through this world wholly oblivious to the aberrant blessings that haunt its borders. But there are individuals among us who, by karmic debt or some other cold twist of fate, lead lives that are hopelessly intertwined with this adumbrated reality, this misshapen plane of existence that thrums beneath the skin of the physical.[19]

But while the tale develops a powerful sense of the bizarre as Neil,

---

[19] Ibid., 61.

apparently deserted by his girlfriend, Kate, finds his mental stability increasingly disturbed by the realization that days have passed without his conscious awareness, the narrative devolves into merely a story of psychological aberration that does not fully account for all the weird elements that have been haphazardly thrown out.

In "Where the Scarab Dwells" Gavin inserts a sociopolitical undercurrent, depicting the comeuppance of a man, Garret, working for a ruthless developer who is evicting poor tenants to erect high-end apartment buildings. Garret is half Egyptian, and his ultimate fate reflects Egyptian tales of the underworld, as he recalls a story told to him by his mother:

> *"Long ago, our dear departed were judged by the deeds they did in the world. But the Egyptian afterlife is different from heaven or hell, son. Going into our underworld, which our ancestors called 'Amenta,' was something that everyone—good people and bad—had to do. It was their final test before they entered Forever. Those who had done cruel things in life would get lost inside Amenta, but the righteous . . . the righteous would have the purity of their hearts to light their way, to guide them until they finally emerged on the far end, like a beautiful butterfly freed from a cocoon of bandages . . ."* [20]

Garret has little doubt what will await him: "When the first shovelful of dirt sprinkled down upon his plastic dressings, Garret became convinced that he would soon be scuttling through a subterranean underworld, helpless as a cockroach in a pipe." But he

---

[20] Ibid., 42.

nonetheless maintains the faith that "he was a good man" and that he would "emerge like a new day sun at the far end of Amenta."[21]

At Fear's Altar begins with a striking prologue ("A Gate of Nerves") that proves to be a brief but powerful vignette about the power of ghost stories. In this volume Gavin expands upon his short-story technique, writing several novelettes or novellas that are among his most compelling works. "The Abject" shows him brilliantly fusing Lovecraftian cosmic horror with an intense focus on the complexity of human relationships. Petra and Tad, a young married couple, agree to go with Charlie and Douglas, a gay couple, to a remote place in British Columbia called Earth's End. Petra, at the edge of a cliff overlooking the Pacific Ocean, sees a needle-like mountain emerging from the water. Charlie tells her that it is called the Abject—and he tells a long tale about the Watchers, alien entities who came to Earth for the purpose of "observing us puny humans as we fumbled our way up the food chain."[22] Later Petra thinks she hears the crying of an infant ("It was the howl of something unwanted, something abject"[23])—could it be the spirit of the child she had just aborted? She steps over the cliff to her death. A year later, Tad returns to the spot and thinks he sees a huge creature emerging from the Abject; Petra, pregnant, is on the creature's wing, and she releases a mewling creature, which flies toward Tad. The tale's relentless narrative pace results in a sense of cumulative horror rarely matched in contemporary weird fiction.

Other stories reflect specific tales by Lovecraft in a somewhat less intense, and at times rather playful, fashion. "Faint Baying from Afar"

---

[21] Ibid., 43.
[22] Richard Gavin, *At Fear's Altar* (New York: Hippocampus Press, 2012), 56.
[23] Ibid., 63.

is an obvious sequel to Lovecraft's "The Hound" (a story that is itself a parody in its over-the-top horror). In the end, Gavin's tale proves to be not much more than a retelling of "The Hound," but it is engaging nonetheless. "The Unbound" is an interesting extrapolation from Lovecraft's "The Unnamable," picking up on one element in that story: can a window preserve some facet of the person who peers out of it for years on end? Here a man starring at an attic window finds that his reflection detaches itself from the window and becomes the Unnamable.

"Only *Enuma Elish*" draws upon the ancient Babylonian legend of Tiamat, who "commands primordial water and winds,"[24] and who was torn in two by her own son, Marduk, but will eventually be made whole. An old woman, Katrina, believes she is Tiamat; and she is in fact killed and dismembered by her son. But when Hurricane Katrina afflicts the Gulf Coast, a neighbor who had helped the old woman ponders on the truth of old legends.

Some stories are so involved that analysis of them is difficult. "The Word-Made Flesh" (the hyphenation is deliberate) is a complex tale of the power of "the Word" to resurrect human beings. "Chapel in the Reeds" is a mesmerizing story that dances between the poles of mental aberration and supernatural menace. An old man, Colin, takes his granddaughter, Toni, into the woods and comes upon an abandoned chapel in a clearing; disturbingly, it is filled with pornographic pictures. They have difficulty finding their way back home, and Paula, Toni's mother and Colin's daughter, is furious that he endangered Toni's life in this manner. There is a clear suggestion that Colin is suffering from the initial stages of Alzheimer's disease; for Colin now remembers that there never was a chapel in the woods.

---

[24] Ibid., 138.

Why, then, does he find the head of Jesus Christ (presumably removed from a crucifix in a chapel) in a nest in a maple tree? Horrifyingly, the expression on the wooden face "was an emblem of rancour, of unfathomable malice."[25] There is more to this story, but its great virtue is its luminous prose, as can be seen in Gavin's description of the chapel that may or may not exist:

> Unbidden, the image of the chapel at night surfaced in Colin's imagination. He pictured it swathed in shadows of the deepest blue, the pitch of its roof and the summit of its steeple knitting with the earthward darkness of the boughs. Cadres of fireflies transformed the lolling reeds into votives. The fetid air was bubbling with the sound of toads and crickets chorusing a chthonic hymn.[26]

"A Pallid Devil, Bearing Cypress" is an anguished tale of wartime Germany, where a man named Josef thinks he once saw the Devil. How else to account for the horrors in which his nation has been plunged? But when he rescues a woman, Helga, from some bombed-out ruins and marries her, he ultimately renounces his interest in the Devil; but Helga, who lets her husband drown in a lake, has a very different view. "King Him" is a grim tale of psychological horror about a man who both impregnates his sister and kills a neighbor's child, all in a quest to bamboozle an evil figure named King Him, who he believes is guiding his actions.

The crown jewel of *At Fear's Altar* is "The Eldritch Faith," a novella of nearly 100 pages dealing with the boyhood, adolescence,

---

[25] Ibid., 42.
[26] Ibid., 37.

and adulthood of a man named Michel. As a child, Michel, playing a game meant to summon ghosts, finds himself confronting a figure named Capricorn. Later, becoming frightened, he traps Capricorn in a music box that serves as a "spirit-trap" and buries him in his backyard. Years later, Michel explores a reputed haunted house called the House of Shades, where he finds a hideous, elephantine old woman. She has the "spirit-trap," and Capricorn is released; Michel ends up killing the old woman. Michel is filled with remorse at ending the life of a fellow human being, and he—as well as the reader—wonders whether Capricorn was really involved at all. But then the body of the old woman is resurrected by Capricorn, who leads Michel into a nebulous realm called Autumnal (first cited in the story "Phantom Passages," in *The Darkly Splendid Realm*):

> Autumnal is not a place, but an eternal moment. It is a state of being where one's innermost nature weds perfectly with some neglected corner of the natural world. Autumnal is smoke and damp air. It is illumined by a slaughtered sun whose rays are filtered through a perennial fog. This is the Greylight; the guttering fallow of the underworld glyphed in the natural world of matter and form.[27]

Michel, who only now realizes that he is a full-grown man, encounters a woman who claims to be his pregnant wife. He tries to kill the fetus but fails; he is confined to a sanitarium. The entire story is in fact a document addressed to his wife; Michel states that the baby

---

[27] Ibid., 237.

"will be an acolyte of an eldritch faith."[28] In effect, "You are carrying Autumnal inside you."[29]

"The Eldritch Faith" is another tale where ambiguity is maintained to the end as to whether the incidents are real or imagined. It features a truly Blackwoodian sense of the ineffable mysteries of Nature and a careful, meticulous dissection of the psychology of terror and weirdness. And it features some of Gavin's most seductive prose:

> The remainder of that summer was enchanting. All through the Dog Days I was blessed by the Bradbury magic of hiding amongst screaming cicadas, of basking under great gunmetal thunderheads as they blotted out the sun, of savouring the shaded circles of sycamores whose boughs hooked Hellward in Reaper-scythe cascades.[30]

Sylvan Dread is a slim collection, its 184 pages bolstered by the reprinting of "Primeval Wood" from *The Darkly Splendid Realm*. As in earlier collections, Gavin is at his best when he portrays conflicted human beings yearning to escape the stifling artificialities of urban life but unprepared to deal with the terrors—real or imagined—presented by the non-human realm of nature. "Tending the Mists" introduces us to a pair of twins, Muni and Zelia, who venture to a remote region where a wedding is to take place. Muni notes that all the guests except the groom appear to be women. Is some hideous sacrifice about to take place—and is Muni herself to be a victim, with her sister suddenly transformed into a goddess? In "Thistle Latch," the narrator

---

[28] Ibid., 252.
[29] Ibid., 253.
[30] Ibid., 207.

tells of a friend he had when he was a child—a boy with the significant name of Lattice Rayburn. When the narrator as an adult has a strange experience in the woods, he seems to realize that Rayburn may have been some sort of trigger that would allow nature to violate its own laws. This tale has a powerfully Blackwoodian atmosphere of terror and awe while yet remaining grimly original.

"Fume" introduces us to a curmudgeon named Clark, who as a permanent resident of the beach resort of Beech Point welcomes the departure of the summer people who flock there. When he comes upon a tent placed in an area where it is illegal to camp, he thinks there is a dead body inside—but it is in fact an effigy of some sort. He stamps on it—and a strange cloud (or "fume") bursts out, going down his throat. This sets the stage for a horrifying scenario where the natural world seems to have invaded Clark's own cottage. "Weaned on Blood"—written for an anthology called *Monk Punk* (2015), which I assume is a volume of horror stories about monks—tells of Brother Baldemar, a Trappist monk, who finds loathsome evidence that a woman from the nearby village is nursing a "stone baby"—a baby that had calcified in her womb, but is in some fashion alive and, worse still, seems to feed on blood. The culmination of this appalling tale must be read to be believed.

"Tinder Row" seems to begin as a tale of urban horror, as it takes us to a remote dead-end street called Tinder Row where the protagonist, Reid, grew up. He meets an old school friend named Agnes after many years. Her life has been marred by tragedy, and out of sympathy Reid takes her to Tinder Row, where she leads him to a copse with a curious human-shaped clearing. What Gavin has done is to draw us insidiously from the comfort of city life to the wilderness that lurks all too close to it—and then he concludes the tale with a cosmic flourish that Lovecraft would have appreciated.

"The Stiles of Palemarsh" is one of Gavin's most successful fusions of emotional tension and supernatural horror. A Canadian named Ian Morrow comes to Wales for what he says is his honeymoon—but he is alone. Twisting his ankle on a jog, he stumbles into a farmhouse, where he claims to the owner that his fiancée, Cari, stood him up at the altar. When the farmer directs him to the road that would take him back to his hotel, Ian finds himself in the midst of bizarre terrors, including a loathsome hermaphroditic entity ("The thing's head was like an overstuffed yard-waste sack. Excess leaves were tugged free by the damp breeze and went flitting off like startled birds."[31]) We later learn that it was Ian who deserted Cari, and, as he becomes increasingly disoriented, he knows that the future bodes ill both for himself and his former beloved.

The novelette that concludes the volume, "Mare's Nest," is endowed with a poignant atmosphere of melancholy that each paragraph augments. When a young woman (she remains nameless, as does her husband) receives some dire but unspecified diagnosis that appears to signal her imminent demise (we are led to assume a malignant and incurable cancer), she compels her husband, a sculptor, to carry through with the promise he had made to her if such a situation were to arise. For many pages we are tantalized by what the couple is actually planning: why does the man first make a papier-mâché figure of a gigantic mare, then spend virtually all his savings on an immense block of black granite? Clearly, we are to understand that the woman is planning her own death—but what will the man's fate be? The ineluctable gloom that descends upon readers as they continue to read, almost against their will, this almost unbearably

---

[31] Richard Gavin, *Sylvan Dread* (n.p.: Three Hands Press, 2016), 151.

intense narrative is a triumph of weird atmosphere.

"A Cavern of Redbrick" tells of a boy, Michael, who comes upon a storage shed in a gravel pit with a strange girl (perhaps made of ice?) sitting on top of it. This bizarre scenario leads to a confrontation with his grandfather, who turns out to be quite other than what Michael thought he was. "Goatsbride" is a luminous prose-poem, although I am not at all clear on the actual thrust or direction of the tale.

Not every tale is a success. "Wormwood Votaries" is an obscure story about a man named Langdon, who as a child experienced some strange visions when he was ill. Beyond that, however, it is difficult to grasp the purpose or intent of the tale. In "The Old Pageant" we find a woman who returns with her fiancé to the cabin she had visited as a child, where her grandmother had played a strange game called the Old Pageant. But the story ends indecisively.

Richard Gavin's five collections of weird tales are a substantial contribution to contemporary weird fiction, infused with conceptions that are complex, original, and richly textured, and expressed in a prose style of singular fluency and lyricism. He has not yet written a novel, but some of his novellas—notably "The Eldritch Faith"— suggest that he would do well in the long form, and there is little doubt of his ability to fashion plots that would require the expansiveness of a novel for their full development. But even if he remains devoted to the short story (with the occasional novelette or novella), every new work of his will be only a further addition to the enviable body of work he has already written.

Bibliography

Gavin, Richard. *At Fear's Altar.* New York: Hippocampus Press, 2012.

— *The Darkly Splendid Realm.* Colusa, CA: Dark Regions Press, 2009.

— *Charnel Wine.* 2004. Rev. ed. Colusa, CA: Dark Regions Press, 2010.

— *Omens.* Poplar Bluff, MO: Mythos Books, 2007.

— *Sylvan Dread.* n.p.: Three Hands Press, 2016.

credit: Aeron Alfrey

The Mad German

By Michael Uhall

THE MAD German makes a dead man's journey across the wasteland where no rivers flow. There are currents of dust moving sinuously across the earth, which itself is as dry and hard as bone. His eyes, weakly blue and fearful, are the only wet things for miles. They slake the thirst of a civilization of flies, but they cannot slake his own.

Death rides this nag of a man.

It was seen clearly by all the inhabitants of the last town in which he stopped before fleeing into the desert. It was seen by young eyes and old when he, his madness apparent, spoke to anyone who would spare him an ear.

He flees the Inquisition, all inquisitions. Those who ask him why he banishes from him with curses. Damn you. Damn you. Damn you.

He reeked of some disease when he first arrived in the town. The town's doctor spared him a bed for a day and tended to him. There were no nurses in the town. As the doctor tended to him, the German hoarsely asked him, Sir, you have some acquaintance with death, I imagine.

The doctor only observed him placidly.

What do you know of the soul?

I am not a priest, the doctor replied.

But you must know of the soul, of its design.

I have heard of it, he said, cleaning his spectacles.

But you have never seen it? Nor touched it? Nor smelled it? Nor tasted it?

No, truly, I have not. The doctor was becoming bored. His thoughts strayed to the company of women.

So, what do you believe happens to the soul after death?

I believe in bodies, the doctor said. When a body dies, it rots, or it becomes so desiccated as to ward off rot.

You are not a religious man, then.

It's true. I am not. I've treated too many bodies, perhaps, the doctor mused.

Do you know the theory of metempsychosis? The German clutched at the doctor's coat, his fingers like crooked sticks. The word comes from the Greek. It means the passage of the soul upon death from a body into another body that yet exists – be it a man or a mare, a tree or a mountain.

The doctor did not know of this word, but, also, he did not much care.

Sleep now, he said, tired of such babble. The Mad German left the doctor's house the next day without speaking another word, even in thanks.

He was remembered by some as the man who drank *pulque* like water and yet who never became drunk. Drunkenness and madness, it seemed, were enemies in him. Never was he seen to touch *mescal*, calling it an impure libation. It was, he said bitterly, far too Spanish a drink for his tastes. The *pulque* he drank instead was harvested by a mysterious and monosyllabic Indian who passed through the town every month and who hid himself and his wives underneath dyed cowls.

In the darkness of the cantina, a young boy often watched the mad German drink the milky beverage. Once, the German beckoned the boy over to him, and he told the following tale in whispers.

This drink is more ancient than the millennia. It is older than men and the dreams given to men. Once, it was the dream of a deity, and long ago the dream was given to the planet by Mayahuel, a beautiful and terrible goddess, for safekeeping. She journeyed into the black desert – for then the land was new, and all deserts were black and only due to time and the machinery of the winds have the sands bleached like old skulls – and she said to the young plant, I give you my dream.

She commanded the young plant to keep her dream a secret from all living things, even from its vegetal brothers.

Flattered, the young plant pledged to obey her, and Mayahuel blessed it. Before she left the earth and retreated back to her superlunary palace, she entreated the young plant to keep her dream safe, and she warned that terrible things would transpire throughout the earth if the young plant failed in its task.

May I not then have spines like my brothers? the young plant asked of her – but she had vanished already into the sky.

Do you know this story already, child, asked the mad German of the boy. He had not.

Still, many ages later, the dream of the goddess Mayahuel remained hidden deep inside the young plant, no longer young.

Early one morning, after a spring storm, two deities passed by the young plant while in the midst of an argument. The two were proud Atlacoya, the goddess of barrenness, and her slinking, spurned lover, Chalchiuhtlatonal, a water god. Chalchiuhtlatonal begged Atlacoya to stay with him, but she looked at him with steely eyes and said that such a love could no longer be, for he had betrayed her with some mortal woman. Then she went from his side.

Chalchiuhtlatonal fell onto a rock near the plant that contained Mayahuel's dream, and he wept bitterly for he was in great torment. After a time, he said to the plant, What must I do to win back the favor of my cold and lovely Atlacoya?

The plant had no suitable reply. Chalchiuhtlatonal became enraged, and he said to the plant, Cursed vegetable! Will you deny your thirst by refusing to advise me? And he kept water from the plant until, parched to the point of death, the plant offered up to him the dream of Mayahuel. So it came to pass that Chalchiuhtlatonal collected the dream into a stone flask.

O sweet dream, he exalted. You will win back for me the favor of my beautiful Atlacoya, and we shall be united again. Chalchiuhtlatonal left the plant in that place, and he sought out Atlacoya. When he found her, he gave her Mayahuel's dream in order to please her and to win back her favor.

But Atlacoya was not pleased by Chalchiuhtlatonal's gift.

For she saw that the dream belonged to Mayahuel, a rival goddess and her antithesis, so she became angry. To Chalchiuhtlatonal, she said, Go from me now and forever. I curse you. For wherever I am, you shall not be. Likewise, wherever you make pool and passage, I shall never be there with you. Then she bound Chalchiuhtlatonal into the forms of rivers and lakes, and his chains were deep canyons and snake-like shores. Even the cloud she enlisted to bind him to the earth. With them, she made an agreement. Whenever Chalchiuhtlatonal would struggle with the clouds, escaping the misted prison they had built for him, the clouds would shout out warnings to Atlacoya with great furor. Whenever he managed to escape, spilling himself onto the ground, Atlacoya would flee to her redoubt in the north.

And Chalchiuhtlatonal wept bitterly, so very bitterly that deluges plagued mankind for an epoch.

You see, child, by this time, mankind had been fashioned. Atlacoya's rage was such that she turned to mankind in order to seek revenge against her former lover Chalchiuhtlatonal and against her hated rival Mayahuel, for Mayahuel was both never-endingly fertile and far more beautiful than Atlacoya could ever hope to be.

So Atlacoya went to visit a man. The man whom she visited was a priest, but he cowered when she approached him, for she was the essence and the visage of bitterness itself. Wherever she went, deserts followed in her footsteps. She said to him, I bring you a gift, priest.

The gift was Mayahuel's dream. It was a cruel gift, for the dreams of deities are not meant for the minds of men. Atlacoya poured the dream over his field so that his crops died and new plants appeared. She taught the priest how to harvest the dream from the plants that grew there and how to prepare it. He imbibed the dream, and, after he did so, he exalted unto the heavens. To thank the goddess Atlacoya, he took his brother into a dry field, where he killed him. Blood for the drought, he said, and his brother's blood sank into the dead ground. Atlacoya loved with great spite the blood that quenched her thirst, for it served to remind her of Chalchiuhtlatonal and the endless agony she had inflicted upon him for his betrayal.

So, she told the priest to quench her thirst often in such a manner. He abandoned the temple of Nanahuatl, a humble god who had sacrificed himself in order to make the sun, and the priest became Atlacoya's most devoted and violent proselyte. Since that time man has been but a servant of the desolation.

There the mad German ended his story. Smacking his cracked lips, he continued to drink from his milky cup.

The boy asked him, But what of Mayahuel? What did she do? What happened to the young plant?

She did nothing. She could do nothing. The deed already was done, and even the gods can't turn back the wheel of time, he said.

The boy asked him, But what was the dream? What was Mayahuel's dream? If she is a kind goddess, then how could her dream be cruel?

Loudly, the mad German laughed in reply. He refused to say anything more. Angered, the boy told no one of their exchange, for it was clear to him that the German had no wits at all.

For six more days, the mad German stayed in the town. Each day he spent in the cantina. It was not known where he spent his nights, although it was rumored that he stayed with a prostitute who tented in a nearby canyon.

He left at midday and headed into the desert tract stretching out like a bleak, unhappy scroll. Some of the town's residents speculated that he planned to meet with anchorites who inhabited the northern tract and who were said to have mastered the secrets of the desert. Others scoffed that there were even such men, or that the mad German would meet them, that such a fool as he could aspire to the rest of hermitage.

When he left the town, his gait was unsteady as if he were drunk, or suffering from some great sorrow. He soon disappeared into the lakes of dust.

Days out, the desert is unkind to him. The sun sits like a sullen burden upon his scorched shoulders. It burns his head, like an angry crown. A dry tongue sits in his mouth behind blackening lips, like a malignant, swollen locust. He even thinks to tear it out for the pain it causes. The heat flogs him. Sand courses through his veins. He is near death.

The mad German believes that nothing at all lives in the desert save the sun, itself a mad beast who does little save despise the terrestrial regions it daily observes. Men in this allotment of the earth sacrifice much to nourish it, the god thing.

The mad German collapses into the dust like a broken stick, staring up into the sky with blank, burned eyes. It hurts to move them. The sun weighs upon him, and he looks into it. Tiny shadows, probably vultures, pass over its face, which he can barely make out through his tears – or, more likely, through the illusion of tears, for such sweet water dare not grace a man's cheek in such heat.

That solar visage opens its mouth, and it speaks to him in the desert with the creaking voice of an aged and indifferent father. Here in his misery it recites to him a passage he knows well.

The sun says, Your foot shall slide in due time, and the day of your calamity is at hand, for those things that come upon you make haste. The mad German gasps for breath, pinned to the earth by these words.

This is what he believes in his last moments, as fevers sweep over his body like the scratching twigs of a coarse broom. There is no veil of sky, he thinks. It has been removed so that the sun can take up my body like some antipodean Elijah. My soul goes, it goes now, into this land.

When the sun stops its susurrating speech, he is still. Flies colonize his body, and coyotes haunt the horizon as the dusk approaches.

Eventually his bones will bleach and become lost.

He becomes one with the desert that shall bear his name.

I Feel Better Now

By Brooke Warra

I'M NOT a junkie, I think as I smash the hammer down on the top of my foot. I know plenty. I've seen 'em. Their crooked jaws always working like they're chewing their words, like words are bubblegum, when they've got their scabby hands out in the parking lots outside of every Sack N Save this side of the county line and always call you dirty names when you keep walking and won't look into their bright eyes or give 'em any money for the use of their little blue cards, the cards meant for feeding all those snotty faces pressed up to the windows of their station wagons. I'm not no goddamn junkie, and I smash the hammer down a second time, and this time I hear it crunch and it's gonna be a pulpy mess if I try once more, and I do try again but my heart's not really in it, so it just makes a soft thud, and I puke.

I was born in a flurry of legs and blood and cusswords in the back of a pizza delivery boy's two-door Honda Civic on the side of the interstate.

The pizza boy had shown up with the two double-cheeses the moment my mother's water broke. They both stood in the doorway of #36 Hollow Drive staring down at the sweet-smelling puddle growing around her bare feet. She wiggled her toes.

"Well, she's early" she said and grabbed him by the collar of his blue polo, "You're taking me to the hospital. I ain't got no one else," and marched him down the stairs.

She squeezed into the back of the car, wedging herself between the seat and the door before popping through. "Jesus H Christ on a crutch," she'd said and motioned for him to put the pizzas in the back with her. In all her thrashing and hollering and rolling around, she would end up giving birth to me on top of two crushed pizza pies, a half-eaten slice stuck to the front of her dress. Five miles from the hospital, she ordered the boy to pull over.

"This baby ain't waiting," she puffed, sweat soaking her hair so that it looked like an oily, black cephalopod clinging to her pale face.

"How do you know? Have you done this before?" he asked, eyes bulging.

"No, but I just touched her head."

The car screeched and swerved to the shoulder, depositing the boy into the path of the oncoming traffic that zoomed past. He ran around to the back, threw the seat forward, tangled himself in the belt, and dove underneath my mother's paisley dress. In the process of delivering me, she would put her foot through the leather of his passenger seat, crack a window, and defecate on the squished pizza boxes beneath her. A slew of foul names escaped her pouty, full mouth and flew at the boy fumbling between her bloody thighs.

"I think it's stuck!" he said, watching my hairy head crown and retreat with a sucking sound.

"Oh, just move out of the way!" she yelled, sat forward, reached her hand inside of herself, and pulled me out by my head.

Years later, my mother would say to me in between drags off a slim, pink cigarette and her oxygen tank, respectively, "And then there you were, glistening and naked in the red and blue lights of the cop car that'd pulled up behind us. All three of us covered in blood," laugh, cough, "We must've been a sight, me, that poor boy, and you—a little ball of silly putty."

After she had yanked me out, the boy had caught and then nearly dropped me, so shocked was he, not just at the sudden squirming proof of life he held in his hands but by my appearance. The cop had approached then, taken one look at the squalling ball of flesh between the two blood-spattered people on the side of the road, made like he was going for the gun at his hip, and then on second glance took his jacket off and wrapped it around the infant, me.

"You're gonna need an escort," he said and instructed the pair to follow him to the hospital.

In the passenger seat a few moments later, my mother finally asked the pizza boy his name.

"Adam," he said and gave my mother a weak smile. Now that the kicking and screaming was over he could see my mother, despite her foul mouth and the stink of loneliness oozing from her pores (and the decade of years she had on him), was a plump, raven-haired, green-eyed beauty.

And that is how I came to be named Eve and how I got a daddy.

But this story isn't about them.

Radial dysplasia and talipes equinovarus are just fancy words for saying you're deformed. When my mother says them, they sound like an incantation, like a spell, like magic. The day I was born, she tells me, my feet were up behind my head, toes (if you could call the webbed nubs at the end of my feet toes) pointed inward, and one arm tucked up by my ribcage, half-formed, like a baby bird's wing.

"Skin like melted candlewax, the day you was born" mother said the first time she told me the story of my origin. I had just stormed home from Sunday school on crooked legs, marched in the door, and demanded to know why I didn't look like the other kids.

I was five and unable to attend public school that year because of the weeks I had spent in the hospital. Up until then, I'd mostly stayed home with Mom and Adam and an elderly neighbor who sometimes babysat me. My mother, who was attending medical assisting courses, taught me to read from her biology books. (At four years old, I had slipped getting out of the bath and whacked my knee on the edge of the tub, and when my parents came running I announced, "I broke my patella!") Adam had suggested I attend Bible study as a way to socialize. Mother, a full-blown heathen, had conceded I needed other children. I needed friends.

The subject of my irregularities had never really come up. My childhood had thus far been a series of corrective surgeries, needles, and stitches, followed by weeks in the hospital and months of recovery. I had made friends, of course, in the hospital. I had met a girl named Anna who was born entirely without legs. And another girl, who had no nose or eyelids, wrote to me regularly. I had never compared myself to other children until that day during recess at church. I had never thought to. The new kids, the normal kids, were quick to teach me how.

She dabbed a cotton ball to the bloody spot on my forehead where a rock, hurled from the hands of the teacher's pet had struck me. "You had limbs just like melted wax the day you was born... But this face," she cupped my chin in her hands, "is the most beautiful face I've ever seen. You was like a angel."

She sighed., grabbed me by the shoulders and looked hard at my face.

"Eve, if God had made you any more perfect it wouldn't be fair to those other kids."

"They hate me!" I wiped my snot on her shirt.

"Well... Fuck 'em." She puffed.

But later she put on her best dress and marched me down the block back to church. While I waited outside on the steps I heard my mother's voice low and scary from the Sunday-school room and only heard Miss Debbie make one quiet peep, which I could tell by her tone was "yes, ma'am," which is the only thing you're allowed to say to mother when she's fired up. After that, I continued to go to Bible study, but the kids didn't throw rocks at me again.

I take the bus to Cleo's house. I can't sit still. I wonder if all the people on their way to work and school from the park-and-ride, busy people saving the planet with their bus passes and shared rides, can see my need. I wonder if I smell like a bitter pill. My skin feels sweaty and like it doesn't fit me right. I can feel every bone in my body. I mean, I am aware of every bone in my body. I wonder if I smell like how I feel. I inch away from the woman cradling a baby next to me. The baby has on a handmade sleepsack, the kind that cinch at the bottom. Its mother is one of those women in soft, creamy clothes with hair that always falls right. They smell like soap and talcum and sour milk. I think they must be on their way to the park. I imagine the mother's mind is a vast, empty space with only thoughts about women's magazine articles, married-sex and casserole recipes floating around. A man across the aisle smiles at me and says something, nodding his head, but I pretend to adjust my headphones so he knows I can't hear him and look out the window and count my bones.

Cleo says the pain meds don't help with her migraines, so she sells them and turns around and buys pot from the neighbor, which she says does help with her headaches. Her house is across town from me, and I take the bus there once a month. Her living room is a confusion of toys and piles of laundry and kids and garbage. I step over a child with a Barbie leg in its mouth.

"Sorry, don't mind the mess, I just don't find the time to clean," she says every time I come over, gesturing at the half a dozen, half-dressed gummy-faced kids on the floor. I have no idea which ones are hers.

"Oh," I say, "You should see my house," and think about the neat stacks of magazines on the coffee table at home and the afghan folded over the sofa arm and the framed photos on the mantle, and feel smug.

We go in the kitchen, and she counts the pills out, holding a baby potato-sack style in the other arm. A radio on the counter blasts static. Ants swarm a puddle of congealed tomato sauce. She pulls the plastic off a pack of cigarettes and sweeps the pills into it. I try to take them from her like I don't really care and throw them in my messenger bag. Now that I have the pills, now that they are in my bag, I feel talkative. She pours me coffee, and I sit in a cracked plastic lawn chair at the dining table. We talk about her husband's job and the crash diet she's on and the kids and the minutiae of her fibromyalgia, and when she's not looking I pop a pill in my mouth and the bitter chalk of it under my tongue sends a carnal shiver down my spine.

For the first several years of my life, before they sliced my tendons to release them, I walked on my tip-toes like a pigeon-toed, one-and-a-half armed ballerina. Adam brought me home little slippers with bows on the end. The leather felt like pale pink flesh and I slipped them onto my scar-riddled feet like new skin.

"What'd you go and do that for?" I heard my mother hiss at him at night. "She ain't never gonna be no dancer."

"You don't know that."

They argued for a long time and that night I dreamed my Achilles tendons were tightly strung violin strings, singing with music with every step I took across the stage before they snapped.

I woke up screaming.

After the surgery, the slippers were gone.

You gotta make sure your bed is made and the fig-flavored candle is burning, and your colored pencils are all lined up next to your sketch pad and you got on your favorite soft pajama pants and your 6-disc cd player is full and on random play and you've got a bowl full of mixed nuts to potentiate the pills you carried home in your pocket inside the wrapper off a pack of cigarettes. You gotta break them all in half, stick a wet finger in the powder that comes off from breaking them and put it on your tongue because you're not wasteful and take a half every fifteen minutes, because otherwise you'll throw up too soon, and it's best to wait before you puke because if you do it at just the right time, afterward you can lay on the bed feeling warm and full and drifting in and out of a dream narrated by Mazzy Starr.

But you ain't no fucking junkie, don't forget that, and if you do just look at all the glossy, angry red scars spoiling your skin.

"It's not so bad," said my second-grade teacher when I told her the kids stuck gum in my hair on the bus and called me a freak.

"It's really not that bad," said the physical therapist when I was relearning to walk after they cut my tendons and fell off the balance beam.

"It's not too bad," the doctor said when he cut open my calf, taking off my cast after my third bone surgery and again after my eighth.

"It's not that bad," the nurse said the day they ripped the metal pins out of my ankles, but she smooths back my hair for me when I start to cry.

"Not bad," my t-ball coach said when I limped along behind the other kids during sprints, patting me on the shoulder and not looking me in the eye. "Not bad at all, E."

"It doesn't hurt that bad," said every LPN that dug around in the crook of my arm and in the skin on the backs of my hands looking for a good stick for the IV. "I've got two-year-olds in oncology that don't cry as much as you."

"You don't have it that bad," the caseworker at the welfare office said. "I saw a girl on the news who only has her thumbs, and she's the most accomplished pianist in the living world."

"Oh, come on, it can't be that bad," mom said when I told her the boys at school shoved my head into my locker, felt up my breasts,

61

and called me a cripple. "No way they did that in front of everyone and no one said anything about it, Eve. Someone would have called me."

But they did. And no one did.

The first time I slammed my fingers in the car door it was an accident. The first time.

Before we bought the house across the river, when we still lived in town and Adam was still delivering pizzas, we rented a five hundred square-foot flat inside a water treatment plant that had been converted into rental apartments. For the first fourteen years of my life, whenever I lie down to go to bed, I stared into the inky blackness of a six-foot lead tube hanging open from the ceiling. The flat reeked of sewage. It got into your clothes, your hair, your pores. The plant sat at the top of the hill on Taylor Street. It was a constant point of contention and an eyesore to the elders and well-to-do from the lower, affluent streets. It squatted, fat and naked, its turbine an anus hovering over the lush landscape dotted by their colonials and townhomes down below. There were annual meetings about what to do with it. Some suggested turning it into an art gallery, painting a mural on the brick exterior. Some suggested blasting or tearing it down. Ultimately, it would remain standing just as it always had since the day it had ceased operation in 1848 and became housing for the less fortunate, down-on-their-luck, and ne'er-do-wells. If you were from "the plant" or even "the top of the hill," the kids down below called you "shithead" and "shitbreath" and "sewer rat" and "Taylor Trash". They made jokes about three-eyed babies and glow-in-the-dark fish.

"Just look at Skeevy Eve," they'd say, jerking their thumbs in my direction, "That's what happened to her," and they'd flap their arms like broken wings, mocking my withered limb even though I did my best to keep it tucked, hidden inside my jacket.

I used my good arm to swing my backpack at their heads.

There was a brief hour of every school day when the Taylor Street kids accepted me as one of their own, and we joined forces against our common enemy, the Saltwater Drive kids. The hour started the minute the last bell rang and lasted through the first half of our bus ride home and after in our hideout among the various discarded items in the lot behind the plant. Abandoned cars, tires, dining room tables, mattresses, any number of suitable materials for proper fort-building lay there. Here, in that rusty wasteland of treasures, we plotted, schemed, and nursed our wounds. In those hazy, golden afternoons, I wasn't One-Armed Eve, or Skeevy Eve, or even Gimp. I was one of them.

It was here, also, that people regularly dumped their unwanted pets, and the junkyard became a breeding ground for feral cats. It was commonplace for the Taylor Street kids to find a nest of newborn kittens and attempt to bring one or all of them home to their parents, who threw them back over the fence, grumbling about mouths to feed.

It was early spring when we found the first litter of kittens. We were on break and hadn't been in school all week. Left alone during the day while most of our parents worked in town, we'd sustained ourselves on popsicles and wild blackberries. So far, we'd had a good run of things; only Tommy from 4b had any injuries when he'd broken his arm falling through the roof of a dilapidated, rusting truck during a no-holds-barred game of king-of-the-hill and there had only been one trashcan fire the day we played "hobo."

I spotted the kitten first, and ran toward it shouting, "Dibs! Dibs! I call dibs!" before any of the other kids could get to it. Jenny (8a), Robin (8b), and Josh (not from the complex but still from Taylor Street) had already gathered around it by the time I limped over.

They stood in a semi-circle staring down at the cat. Before I could wonder aloud why no one had tried to pick it up, all three of them took a step backwards, away from the cat, in unison.

"What—" I started to ask but then saw the kitten fall over to the side, struggle to right itself, take two steps, and fall again.

"I don't think we should touch it," Jenny said, subconsciously wiping her hands on her corduroys as if to clean them.

"What's wrong with it?" Robin asked. She took another step back.

The kitten was wandering in circles now. It was a gray ball of fluff. Too young to be away from its mother, really. Its mouth opened and closed but no sound came.

"Aw, she needs her mom," I said. "We should take her to her mom."

I bent down to scoop the cat up with my good hand and all three of the other kids shouted: "Don't!"

But I already held her in the crook of my arm. Up close, I could see the faint markings of stripes in her fur. Her eyes were a coagulated milky color. No irises. They bulged from her face. Her jaw worked, snapping open and closed.

The rest came to me all at once, in slow motion, and too late. Afterward, I would run home, retching and crying for a long time in the shower.

A tiny, protruding rib, as delicate and sharp as a fish bone. No teeth, no tongue inside the yawning mouth. No pink, wet nose just a raw bone. In her skull, a gaping wound. Inside the wound, dozens of squirming maggots. They were behind her swollen eyes, in her ears, wriggling through her fur.

I dropped the kitten and began to sob, sucking in great gulps of air. She lay there, stunned, then after some struggle, clawed her way upright and began walking in endless circles again. A bag of maggots staggering around in a kitten suit.

Sometimes, I dreamed my skin was full of larvae. I would feel them writhing around, tunneling through my cartilage, creeping along the wrinkles in my brain, oozing out of my pores. I would wake up crying, even at twenty-years-old, crawling into my mother's lap in the middle of the night. She was usually still up reading. I don't know that I ever saw my mother sleep.

No one would have guessed, but my mother was an avid reader, devouring paperbacks, consuming texts, demolishing reference books. They lined the walls, held up the furniture, crowded the kitchen counters. You'd trip over them in the dark on your way to the bathroom. She talks like a hick, but I've heard her intellectually devastate anyone who condescended to her. My earliest memories are of being gently rocked in her lap while she read to me from medical dictionaries and literary classics. I never owned a picture book.

On the bad dream nights, she would cradle me and put her lips to my ear, whispering, "You're okay, you're okay, shshshsh, you're okay."

I'd bury my face in the skin of her neck where she smelled like cigarettes and lotion and howl, "There's something inside of me."

"There's something inside of me!" I scream when I'm waking up in the recovery room after surgery. My bones feel wrong, like my skin is stretched over the wrong skeleton, like I was shoved into the wrong sack of flesh.

Mom and the nurses rush to me.

"What's happening to me?" I grab my mother's shirt.

There are hands all over me. I wonder if they're pushing my bones back inside. A nurse taps a syringe and injects something into the IV at my wrist. Before I can scream again, the medicine takes hold. Their faces hover above me. My mother looks scared.

"Do you know who I am?" I try to ask her, but I pass out.

"I don't know who you are anymore, Eve," Adam says.

He's found my stash of pills. Not the kind that come in the little orange bottles with proper labels on them. He's found the baggie of crushed powder hidden inside the trinket box he carved for me for my thirteenth birthday. The one he'd made for the birthstone ring he'd saved up for a year to buy me. The ring he bought with a year's worth of skipping his morning coffee and returning aluminum cans, cans he picked out of public dumpsters and collected off the side of the road. He'd given me the ring inside the handmade box with a note written in his shaky script that said: "I am so proud of the young lady you have become."

He throws the baggie at me. I catch it and hug it to my chest.

"You're not my fucking dad, Adam," I say and roll my eyes like an insolent child. I'm not. I'm twenty-five. I still live in his house.

Adam, who's never even yelled at me, takes a step forward, and I think he might hit me. I once set the living room carpet on fire playing with some firecrackers when I was home alone, and he didn't hit me then. Now, instead, he balls his fists at his sides and stares at me for a long time without speaking. I think of him running behind me on my first big-girl bike. I think of him reading to me in the hospital and bringing me a stuffed bear after every surgery. The bears line the perimeter of my room now. I think of the time mom locked me out of the house in the heat of an argument and how Adam picked me up and drove me around for an hour, buying me a strawberry soda and letting me pick the radio station.

I wish he would say something.

I wish he would hit me.

Mom slaps me across the face, hard. She bursts into tears. She's caught me hammering at my foot. But she drives me to the hospital and fights with the doctors when they say they won't give me painkillers and offer me ibuprofen instead.

"My child is in pain," she says through gritted teeth. She is a foot taller than she normally is and there's fire in her eyes.

She drives me to every urgent care in the county until we find a doctor who barely looks up from his prescription pad to examine me.

He writes a note for the painkillers and another for an antipsychotic. We pick them up at a pharmacy we haven't used before. They rattle inside their bottles, the bottles rustle against the white paper bag, it's like a beat along with the music on the radio. I clutch the bag in my lap. I feel upbeat. My foot throbs, and I remind myself that it hurts, and I need the pills because it hurts. I can't wear a shoe for a month.

The pills slide inside the bag when we turn corners, whispering.

Mom and I don't talk on the way home. Before I get out of the car she asks me, "What's happening to you, Eve?" but I slam the door.

I resolve to only take the pills when I need them. I give the trinket box to mom and Adam, knocking on their door at bedtime, sheepishly holding the box out to them. They are in bed in their pajamas, each with a book in their lap. They let me talk for a long time. Finally, Adam takes the box from me.

"Thank you for being honest, Eve," he says.

"Yes, thank you," mother says, and she pats the edge of the bed, so I sit down, and she hugs me tight.

"I'll only take them when you say it's time," I assure them for the hundredth time. They nod and give me tired smiles. We're all in agreement. I feel relieved. I've slipped out of a pair of handcuffs that have had me shackled to that little box, bound to the ceremony of cracking the lid, counting the pills, breaking them into smaller and smaller pieces until I'm licking powder off my fingers. Chained to—

"I'm not a pill-head. I'm not a junkie. I would admit it if I was, you know that, I'd be the first to say it," I'm babbling. My mother rubs my back as I talk.

"Of course, sugar," she says. I sense their eyes meeting over my head. Adam is mouthing something to my mother, his hands are gesticulating. I feel her shake her head, no.

I make apologies and promises. We all do. I go to bed determined to keep them. We all do.

Two days later, I pick the lock on their bedroom door while they're at work and take back the box.

No one says anything.

The doctor held up each of my dozen x-rays to the light, flipped them over, turned them sideways, shuffled them in their pile, and sighed. I was seventeen and we were planning for my final corrective surgery. We were running out of experts, running out of innovative ideas, running out of insurance. She is the last in a series of specialists I will see throughout my life.

"I'm not gonna lie to you," she said.

"Please don't."

She misunderstands me and continued, "You probably won't be much better off after this surgery, to be perfectly frank."

When I start to cry she doesn't offer me a tissue, doesn't tell me to look on the bright side, doesn't say it could be worse. She looks at me and says, "It sucks, kiddo."

We talk about the reasons to go ahead with the surgery. It's experimental, new to the states, she's never performed it before.

"It won't make you better, Eve," she said. "But I believe you will retain the ability to walk longer than you would have without it."

I had never considered the possibility that I would lose my ability to walk. It had never occurred to me. Before I could respond she said:

"Well, I've got another patient waiting. Twenty-four of you today! Can you believe it? The day after Thanksgiving! It gets crazy around here," and she scratched out a note on her prescription pad. "Here, before I forget, pick these up on your way home. They'll help with the pain."

She left, and I sat for a long time on the exam table in the paper gown, gripping the little square of paper in my hand, listening to the clock on the wall tick the seconds.

We were halfway home before I loosened my grip and unfolded the paper, smoothing it out on my leg.

"Oh, mom, the doctor says I should take these."

"Try this stuff, let me know if you want more," Cleo says and hands me a baggie and slaps at a bug that isn't on her arm. She laughs. "Little fuckers are eating me alive."

Credit: Yves Tourigny

I've been staring at myself in the mirror for three going on four days. I have to watch my eyes. If I look away, I can feel them staring at the top of my head. If I fall asleep, right here, in front of this mirror, they'll still be in the reflection, wide open and watching me. I keep trying to catch them at it. I slide my eyes, my real ones, to the side, pretend I'm real interested in the wall or my shoe or the fly buzzing around my room and then jerk my gaze fast back to the mirror. From the corner of my eye, forty-some-odd hours ago, I caught myself smiling at myself. All night last night I locked eyes with the girl in the mirror and dragged a razor I pried out of its yellow plastic casing across my skin, just to see what she would do. She didn't even flinch. That was a clue. I would have screamed if someone slashed me up and down my arms and legs like that. She didn't. I can't stand the sight and smell of blood. I would've passed out at the sight of all that blood soaking into my bra and shorts. She didn't. I try screaming in her face, but she doesn't let on that she knows I know what she's doing.

I have to keep watching her.

I smash the palm of my hand right in her fucking face, and the mirror shatters, and now there are a dozen shards of glass in a spiral, and she's got three sets of eyes, and some of them are where her cheek should be, where her neck should be. I lean in close and my breath fogs up the reflection.

"Open your mouth," I whisper.

She does and inside, in the black hole of her throat, deep inside, an eye opens and rolls wildly before looking directly at me.

I try to scream but something is crowding my mouth. I'm afraid to look, but I do. I look into the splinter of mirror again. I open my mouth wide and the eye is gone.

I'm choking.

I can't breathe, and something is clawing at my throat, at my tongue, cramming into my mouth. I tilt my head back and grab my jaw and pull down to get a better look. Ten fingers reach out, two hands emerging, gripping the sides of my face, and she's tearing her way out of me, tearing me apart.

I feel better now.

credit: Toni Tošić

The Glow at Home

By Rayna Waxhead

EVERYTHING HAD bumps and lumps, scratches and ridges: the walls, the floor, the itchy clothes the men with guns gave us, their discolored distorted faces, and now my once perfect and creamy-smooth skin. I was scratched, bruised, banged and bumpy from being taken with the others. Were the men with guns trying to turn us into one of them? Were they trying to give us their same muddled faces? Everything around me was dark and muddled too. Shadows clung to every corner in the room, hung under every tired eye, and lined the large table we sat at. Would skeletons jump out and sing and dance?

I missed the glowing smooth face of Big Mother and the perfect, unbroken, white walls of home where there were no shadows. And I missed the glow of my cartoons too. Where were the cartoons in this place?

The food was bumpy and lumpy and brown too. "Oatmeal" — what was that? Where was the Cushion Toast or the Real-Meat Gummy Burgers? Where were the Cheese Shakes and the Chocolate Pizza? And why was this "oatmeal" served in a heavy bowl instead of a clean plastic package?

The others around the table ate the slop. Were they afraid of the men with guns? Big Mother always told me to listen to men with guns. And when I accidentally watched Wrong Channel I saw guns make a woman's head go splat. I was afraid, but the oatmeal looked like puke, so I only drank the milk. It was white and smooth and pure, and Big Mother said it makes you grow big like her.

A man with guns, the one with a red hat, stood up and cleared his throat. "If you're done eating, please line up to wash your dishes in the basin."

I looked to the others, and their faces mirrored my confusion. The red hat man continued, "In the real world, food and plates aren't thrown away. They don't just disappear. Washing dishes is what's called a chore. You'll be learning how to do other chores too. You'll grow and prepare your own food. You'll learn to keep a home. And one day you'll take pride in doing these chores. Chores are what real people do to be self-sufficient and live on their own."

Live on my own? Why? I didn't want to live on my own. I wanted Big Mother and her helpers. I wanted to go back to the shiny smooth white home with the cartoons. I wanted the glow.

The red hat man looked to us, and when we didn't react, he broke the confused silence by striking the butt of his rifle on the table. We all shuffled into a line in front of the basin to the sound of the echoing thump.

As I got closer to the sink, a man with guns approached me. It was a woman with long dark hair and dark skin. "It looks like you didn't even touch your oatmeal. Did you try it?"

I shook my head "no" ever so slightly. The dark woman picked up the spoon from my bowl and scooped up some of the gunk. She faked a smile and held it in front of my mouth. "Aahhh," she said, like Big Mother when I was a baby. I wasn't a baby. I was a big girl, twenty years old!

I shook my head "no" again. Her smile dropped as she sighed. She gripped the sides of my jaw and squeezed, forcing it open to accept the slop she shoveled in. "This is what real food tastes like."

Real food was disgusting. It sat on my tongue like it was partially chewed, some bits like jelly and others stiff. I spat it out all over my scratchy rough clothes and dropped the bowl on the floor.

The dark woman picked up my bowl. She handed it to me and led me to the sink. "You'll learn to like it. And it's good for you, too."

The dark woman shoved a smelly wet thing in my hand. I dropped it into the sink immediately. She picked the squishy square back up and forced it into my grip, taking my hand and moving it in circles to wipe the oatmeal off the bowl and into the basin. She looked up at the red hat man. "This one's going to be quite a project."

He chuckled. Not a happy chuckle—a chuckle like Big Mother would make before she punished me. He looked at me. "We wash our dishes so we can use them again."

Use that bowl again? How could it be clean? Why wasn't the oatmeal in a clean smooth package I can put in the trash slot when I'm done?

The red hat man waved me over. "Sarah, we have you down for

milking the cow with John."

"That's not my name," I said, keeping my head lowered.

"It is now. A new name is important for your transition. Now, do you know what a cow is?"

I smiled and nodded my head quickly. A cow was a friendly character who sings and dances and you pull on to get milk. Cows were in cartoons. My favorite cartoon. Finally, I knew something. "Are we on a farm?"

"I knew you weren't hopeless! Yes Sarah, we're on a farm."

A farm was a friendly place with a lot of funny animal friends, I knew that.

The red hat man paired me up with one of the others, John, and another man with guns, one with a way too big nose. The big nosed man led us to the front door. I skipped toward it, ready to see the farm. Farms had bright green, fluffy, round trees, perfect, straight, brown fences. The floor was bright green or brown but not muddled. And very smooth too, no lumps or bumps. Farms had nice blue-sky walls with bunches of white circles painted on them. And animal friends! Nice, smooth, fluffy friends.

But what I saw when I ran out was nothing like my cartoons. The floor was one million—I could never count so many—green and brown spikes, sticking out like doctor's needles or broken screen-glass. A thousand different greens and yellows and browns were all muddled together. The trees weren't fluffy, they were twisted and had sharp little green pieces all over them, and they wouldn't keep still. And the walls, I couldn't tell where they were. And when I looked up I couldn't tell where the ceiling stopped and where it connected to the walls. It was all so far away, the room was so so big and the sun was so bright and warm.

The sky wasn't a wall. It never stopped. There were no walls, there was no ceiling! I looked down, trying to keep my balance. If I looked up I might float up forever. The big nosed man put his hand on my shoulder. "Have you never been outside before?"

He forced my head up. "It's okay, see? It can't hurt you. It's beautiful."

The world began to spin around, and I went limp in his hands. It spun and spun until I passed out.

I cracked my eyes open. Where was I? So tired. Dizzy. I was lying in a bed. It wasn't as soft as my marshmallow bed at home but not as hard as the bunk bed that hurt my back here. The glow, I saw the glow. It was just a faint line on the floor. I slid off the bed on to the dirty floor and crawled to meet the glow. It was shining from under a door. Did they have cartoons in there? Was my room hiding behind this door all along? No, it couldn't have been. I pressed my face against the gap under the door, trying to see into the room. All I could see was the glow flickering on the floor.

Strong hands lifted me up and placed me back on the bed. I didn't resist. I was tired, so tired. I looked up. "Are there cartoons?"

"I'm sorry, Sarah. No cartoons."

My eyes lost focus on the face of the red hat man and closed as I slipped into sleep.

They called them "potatoes," and they were rough and lumpy looking, like everything else in the "real world." My chore that day was to peel them. They were hard and felt like soap under their rough, muddled-brown skin. The men with guns said to throw out the green ones because they could be poisonous, like a black bottle with skull and crossbones on it. I couldn't believe we'd eat something so hard and soapy tonight.

I went outside that morning. The sun felt nice on my skin, like a thin, warm blanket, and I was getting used to its brightness. But I still couldn't look up into the no-wall sky for very long. The air blowing on my skin tickled my arms and made me smile. The air smelled good too, like the air fresheners Big Mother sprayed, but easier to breathe. And I smelled a real flower too. A daisy.

I missed Big Mother. I missed her brushing my hair, covering my skin with lotion, and the games we played. Sometimes she gave me candies when I played the games right and showed me off to her friends, the other big mothers. I missed the candies. Did they have candies in the real world?

My thought bubble burst and I cut my finger with the peeler. Blood dripped out, and I screamed. Blood is bad. I saw it on Wrong Channel. The red hat man came and took me away to another room, the one I slept in when I got sick. He sat me down on the bed and poured stinging liquid onto my finger and covered it with a bandage. I cried and cried.

"It's okay," he said.

I couldn't look up at him. "I'm scared. I want to go home," I said through tears.

"You're safe here," he said, "Look at me."

He took off his hat and bent down and parted his hair to show me two extra kitty-ears—his mod. "I haven't had the courage to remove them yet."

He moved his hand down to his belt and tugged on it. "And down here, smooth, no lumps or holes, like a doll. Just like you. But now I'm a real person."

Behind him, across the hall the door opened, the door with the glow. I glimpsed a lot of glowing screens. Did they have cartoons on any them? I couldn't tell, but I knew I had to find out.

The potatoes tasted good when they were cooked, not hard and soapy. They were crunchy on the outside but fluffy inside. Like a candy shell with chewy chocolate but rougher. But the roughness made it more crunchy. And I could eat more than candies because it didn't make me feel sick.

But the candy was still better, and my room was better than this place. It had Big Mother and my cartoons. Maybe if I went to the sick room again, I could sneak into the room with the cartoons. Maybe if I ate enough green potatoes I could get sick.

They thought I was sick. I knocked over the big nosed man and bolted into the room with the glow. But there weren't any cartoons. There were screens with videos of different places on the farm, one of them a video of the men with guns right outside the room trying to get in. They were scrambling and calling to each other and banging on the door. And there were videos of men and women in suits and ties talking with words scrolling below them. And there was a video with a picture of me, with my real name, "BUBBLES" above it and "LOST" underneath. The picture changed to show one of the others, and below the changing pictures it said, "If you've seen any of these pets call Pet Control immediately." And there was a number. I picked up the phone on the table and pressed the numbers on the screen. The voice said to stay on the phone, said that they were tracing my location and that they're coming.

The sound of a gun struck the door. The red hat man kicked it open and ran in with the other men with guns. I was still holding the phone. He grabbed it and slammed it down. The dark woman grabbed my shirt, her face up to mine. "Who did you call? Who did you call?"

"They're coming," I said.

The men with guns were running, running around the farm and gathering the others. They lined them up and put them in the same van they took us with. The red hat man grabbed my hand and pulled me towards the van. "Come on! We have to get out of here!"

The dark woman separated us. "Just leave her behind! She's caused us enough trouble."

"We don't leave anyone behind. Remember why we do this."

He grabbed me, shoved me into the van with the others and slammed the double-doors shut. We were all so scared, shaking with the bumpy ride away from the farm.

"What's happening?" said John.

The others were all looking at me. "They're coming. They're coming to take us home."

"I don't want to go home! My Big Mother touches me," said another.

And another: "I like real food and real air!"

"I don't have to do tricks here. What I do, I do for myself. And for us," said John.

The van swerved with a screech and spun out of control. We all tumbled to one side of the van, and our limbs tangled together and were crushed under the weight of each other.

We heard a torrent of chaos surround the van, shouts and gunfire and screams attacked the walls until it was as silent outside as it was inside. The doors were wrenched open and men with guns—different men, bigger guns and helmets—reached in and tore us out of our hiding. They wore blue jumpsuits with a yellow badge that read "Pet Control."

The red hat man, the dark woman, the big nosed man, and the other men with guns all lay on the floor outside the van, full of holes and covered in blood. Just like Wrong Channel. Big Mother said never watch Wrong Channel. Blood is bad. I looked away.

The others screamed and cried and thrashed. I didn't resist, but they bruised and pulled and slapped me too. They pulled my arms back and tied my wrists together and banged my head on the door as

I was shoved into another van.

After a bumpy ride, they took us to a gray room. They cut and ripped off our clothes, squeezed and pinched our bodies, and sprayed us with a hose. The water was freezing. They gave us new clothes, bungee pants and baggy white shirts and cut the ties off our wrists that left a red mark of broken skin.

Big Mother finally came. She rushed to me with tears in her eyes. "Bubbles, what did they do to you?" Her hug was too tight, her squishy body pressed against mine, surrounding me against my tender bruised body. She smelled so strong, too sweet, like the flowers in the farm but shoved into my nose. She thanked the Pet Control men and took me to home. "Let's go home, I'll play your favorite cartoon." My glowing cartoons. I was going home. The comfortable, smooth, cozy, not lumpy or bumpy home.

My room was smaller than I remembered, not much space to move around. The walls were smooth but bare, blank. No muddled colors, but no colors at all. Why did it feel so empty? The light felt cold, and the air felt thin.

"Let me put on your favorite cartoon," said Big Mother, sitting me down on her lap, engulfing me in her soft body.

Yes! My cartoons. My favorite cartoon filled the wall screen. The show played on a loop over and over while I ate candies and Big Mother stroked my hair.

The cartoon farm looked lifeless. The colors were too cold and bright. They stung my eyes. The animal's songs hurt my ears. My stomach hurt, and my tongue was sore from the candy.

"I almost forgot," said Big Mother, "Let me hook you up."

I felt a tingle in my back-port, and warmth began to fill my body. The stinging on my tongue faded, and my eyes relaxed, sinking into the light. The cartoons came back to life, the bright colors became warm and inviting again, the high pitch of farm animal's songs calmed my mind, and the room grew and glowed. The glow was home.

The Ghosts of their Guns: Magical Realism in the Fiction of Nadia Bulkin

By S. L. Edwards

I.

THE SOCIAL scientist Benedict Anderson conceived of nations as "imagined communities," things which are at once imagined by those who believe in them while also having real power because of this collective belief.[1] For Anderson and other social scientists, studying the concept of the nation, the idea that the nation is a fabrication does not lessen the potency of group identity. The nation, defined as a group of people sharing a common identity, and the state, defined as a bureaucracy with governing powers within

---

[1] Benedict Anderson, *Imagined Communities: Reflections on the Origin and Spread of Nationalism* (New York: Verso Books, 2006), 6.

a given territory, have extensive and measurable influence over the lives of its members.[2] The state (or nation-state) is an omni-present framework, rippling into the lives of every actor within its borders, even though these borders are imaginary.

Nadia Bulkin has been rightly credited with placing her background in political science in dialog with her fiction. Reading "Intertropical Convergence Zone" is reading the history of both a state (Indonesia) and the ideological underpinnings of the Suharto dictatorship.[3] Told through the point of view of a member of Indonesia's Armed Forces, "Intertropical Convergence Zone" is an allegorical tale about Suharto's ascent to the presidency and the foundation of archipelagic unity (Pancasila). It is the first story in the author's debut collection, *She Said Destroy*, and acts as something of a mission statement.

Though he is never the main character in any of the stories, the specter of Suharto is the most present monster across Bulkin's ghost tragedies. The politics and legacy of his dictatorship inform worlds that seem realistic and believable, though one may encounter the stray ghost or demon in them. Such encounters are rarely met with the sort of hypochondriac reaction one might find in a Lovecraftian character facing "unnamable horror." Instead, these characters react with a certain poise and resolve, as if what they are experiencing is part of a routine and everyday existence. And it is *in* the routineness and the realness of these interactions between characters and the supernatural forces that the *horror* of Bulkin's stories comes through.

Stylistically, there is no denying Bulkin's mastery of horror. But in the near universal accolades her work has received (at the time of

---

[2] Ibid.

[3] Nadia Bulkin, *She Said Destroy* (Petaluma: Word Horde, 2017).

writing, *She Said Destroy* is a finalist for the Shirley Jackson Award) an analysis of how these stories adopt techniques and characteristics of magical realism has been absent. Magical realism, associated with writers such as Jorge Luis Borges, Julio Cortázar, Gabriel García Márquez and Salman Rushdie, has seen a multitude of often conflicting definitions. The term was first coined by Andrea Flores in her analysis of Latin American literature, and as such "magical realism" has come to be associated predominately with Latin America.[4] This analysis will use a definition paraphrased from Maggie Ann Bowers, who defines magical realism as a type of fiction in which a highly-detailed, realistic setting is populated and invaded by characters and events that are too hard to believe.[5]

Bulkin's fiction certainly fits this bill. In *She Says Destroy* there are ghosts who come back from the dead as a matter of fact. There are demons who haunt family lines, and such information does not unnerve, horrify or otherwise propel those who encounter them to run away as if from an incomprehensible terror. These ghosts are simply part of the world, and this is especially true for the role of the state in Bulkin's fiction. The presence of the Suharto dictatorship across her fiction is comparable to the presence of political violence in the works of Gabriel García Márquez, Borges and other magical realists. In Bulkin's fiction, politics and the Suharto dictatorship inform a believable setting where ghosts are as real as the violence that made them, demonstrating how the concept of the imagined community creates a very real and very familiar world.

This essay will seek to place Bulkin's fiction in dialog with other

---

[4] Angel Flores, "Magical Realism in Spanish American Fiction," *Hispania* vol. 38, no. 2, 1955 (Baltimore: The American Association of Teachers of Spanish and Portuguese), 187–192.

[5] Maggie Ann Bowers, *Magic(al) Realism* (New York: Routledge: 2004), 3.

magical realists' works. The following section will offer a more general comparison and analysis of her fiction and that of other magical realists. The third section will offer a more specific comparison of the magical realism of *She Said Destroy* and *100 Years of Solitude*. Both works use politics and history to inform a world which feels lived-in and relatable. The legacies of repression, civil war, and widespread violence allow the horrors of both Bulkin and Márquez to cut deeper than they would otherwise. As such, Bulkin's ghosts are much like Benedict Anderson's imagined communities: they are not real, but they are no less terrifying for it.

II.

"There was a time when I thought a great deal about the axolotls. I went to see them in the aquarium at the Jardin des Plantes and stayed for hours watching them, observing their immobility, their faint movements. Now I am an axolotl."- Julio Cortázar, "Axolotl."[6]

The narrator of Julio Cortázar's "Axolotl" begins telling his story in a very normal fashion.

I was fond of axolotls. I was obsessed with axolotls.

Now I *am* an axolotl.

The characters of Bulkin's "Live Through This" likewise treat the supernatural in a cool, nonchalant manner. When the body of Danielle Haas reappears "cold and clean," the sheriff's department

---

[6] Julio Cortázar, *End of the Game and Other Stories* (New York: Harper Colophon Books, 1978), 3.

conducts an investigation.[7] When the body presumably begins killing people, the town does not react by burning the corpse or by calling an exorcist or the national guard.[8] Rather, somewhat reminiscent of Shirley Jackson's "The Lottery," the citizens of Iram's Hill instead opt to "share the burden" and take in Danielle's corpse for month-long shifts. Throughout the story, residents live with an unusual ghost who is essentially a loaded gun that could fire at random, and in doing so normalize the presence of a character who would otherwise be "otherworldly."

Danielle Haas is not the only ghost whose presence seems routine in Bulkin's fiction. In "The Five Stages of Grief," a ghost by the name of Matilda exists in a world where those who die are either "Benigns" or "Bleeders."[9] Both "Benigns" and "Bleeders" are a part of everyday life in this world, and though Matilda's lingering amongst her living family is horrifying, it is not treated as a reality-defying event. Both the town of Manfield and the eerie ability of neighboring children to hold their breath for seven minutes are normal in the superbly magical realist story "Seven Minutes in Heaven."[10] In "Girl, I Love You" curses and spirits alike are both acknowledged by an unnamed government which treats them in a manner comparable to how real governments treat diseases.[11] Just as real governments warn about the spreads of disease through announcements which warn people to avoid certain practices and foods, the state in "Girl, I Love You" warns

---

[7] Nadia Bulkin, *She Said Destroy* (Petaluma: Word Horde, 2017).

[8] Ibid.

[9] Ibid.

[10] This story is particularly characteristic of magical realism in that it does not adhere to a strictly linear interpretation of time, though characteristics of a bildungsroman are certainly present. The story meanders and defies realistic standards all the more for it.

[11] Nadia Bulkin, *She Said Destroy* (Petaluma: Word Horde, 2017).

its populace about what causes curses and what can be done to prevent them. For this unnamed state government, ghosts are just another sort of disease.

Like the transformation of Cortázar's narrator into an axolotl, the supernatural in Bulkin's fiction is an interruption of reality rather than a break from it. It is not treated as a departure from the real world, but rather an extension of it. Characters continue going to work, continue coming of age and forming relationships despite the corpses in their living rooms. Much like the ghosts of Prudencio Aguilar and Jose Arcadio Buendía in *100 Years of Solitude*, these ghosts often symbolize more relatable and powerful horrors. And like the Buendías, Bulkin's characters treat these ghosts more like unwelcome guests than objects of terror.

Life in the magical realist world continues alongside the supernatural. As it is a normal and everyday part of the world, there is no such concept as the "otherworldly." The characters do not react as we would upon encountering the unbelievably strange for the first time. They have grown up with it and consequently find nothing unbelievable about the unbelievable at all. This is true for Bulkin's characters, who act in direct defiance of the idea that the horror of a monster ends once it is revealed. Rather, in the light of day, clear and visible and no longer "other," the terror of such a thing is much greater. In this way, Bulkin melds the routine of magical realism with the bite of horror in a brilliant and distinct manner.

The result are monsters which are greater than any traditional demon, more real and relatable than a shambling otherworldly darkness. And among these very real, very personal monsters, one stands with the most looming shadow:

Suharto.

III.

Indonesia is unique among nations in that its military predated the foundation of the nation itself. For this reason, the military has always placed itself in a position of privilege and importance relative to other political forces. At the end of WWII, the TNI (the acronym for the Indonesian military at the time) only reluctantly accepted the presidency of the prominent nationalist Sukarno.[12] However, the end of the second war saw the return of Dutch colonizers, who promptly recaptured Sukarno in 1949.[13]

It was an embarrassment the army would not forgive.

And this was true of one lieutenant-colonel leading the TNI guerrilla campaign against the Dutch.

A man who would become General Suharto.

Suharto would support the Sukarno regime, even as the president assassinated and imprisoned political opponents. The straw that broke the camel's back came towards the regime's end, when Sukarno was implicated in fomenting divisions within the military and in the murders of six senior army generals.[14] A coup emerged, and when the smoke cleared Suharto had assumed control of Indonesia's government.

This is the background of the events of "Intertropical Convergence Zone," a symbolic and magical retelling of the foundations of the Suharto dictatorship and the creation of a national myth. In it an unnamed lieutenant provides an unnamed general

---

[12] Sergio Bitar and Abraham F. Lowenthal, eds., *Democratic Transitions: Conversations with World Leaders* (Baltimore: John Hopkins University Press, 2015), 38.
[13] Ibid., 139.
[14] Ibid., 140.

(though there is every reason to believe this is Suharto) items to consume, such as knives and bullets, that will allow him to assume enough supernatural strength to rule his country.[15] The lieutenant's justification for the increasingly gruesome sacrifices that come with these objects is telling:

> It [the sacrifice] was for the General, so, okay. I love this country, and Communism's a Satan and the President's its lackey...We need a man like the General, an honest man. He's one of us.[16]

The allegation that Sukarno was colluding with communists was a common one prior to the end of his regime, despite the massacre of communist party sympathizers in 1965.[17] The general's consumption of these magical items also appears to be an allusion to one of the ideological pillars of Suharto's dictatorship, Pancasila. The idea, originally from the Sukarno era, consisted of five ideological tenants: "(1) belief in one God, (2) just and civilized humanity, (3) unity of Indonesia, (4) democracy guided by the inner wisdom in unanimity arising out of deliberation among representatives, and (5) social justice for all the people of Indonesia."[18]

Suharto's dictatorship came to emphasize the third point of Pancasila above all others, and maintaining archipelagic unity became

---

[15] Nadia Bulkin, *She Said Destroy* (Petaluma: Word Horde, 2017).

[16] Ibid.

[17] Sukarno's involvement in this massacre is still debated. However, there is more than compelling evidence to suggest that by 1965 Sukarno had lost control of an already relatively fragmented military, and that the TNI carried out this massacre without the involvement or knowledge of the President.

[18] Sergio Bitar and Abraham F. Lowenthal, eds., *Democratic Transitions: Conversations with World Leaders* (Baltimore: John Hopkins University Press, 2015), 138.

the primary mission. The General's consumption of magical items from across the archipelago symbolizes this unity, the creation of an imagined community. That many of the consumed items (knives, bullets from the heart of communists, etc.) are associated with violence symbolizes the price the Suharto regime believed it had to pay for this archipelagic unity. The maintenance of the regime entailed brutal campaigns of counter-insurgency, purges, and the severe restriction of social liberties. Ethnic minority groups such as the Acehnese became targets of the dictatorship, and in 1975 the regime undertook an invasion of newly-independent East Timor. Fears of separatism and communist infiltration guided the regime's repression, and Suharto held on to power until 1998. Though he is not a well-known dictator, particularly in the west, Suharto *was* a tyrant. His regime was responsible for mass killings and countless unmarked mass graves. It is likely that we will never know the whole scope of his regime's crimes, as the General died in 2008 never having stood trial for the abuses of his regime.[19]

If "Intertropical Convergence Zone" is the regime's foundation, other stories allow a brief glimpse into life under Suharto. The masterful "Red Goat, Black Goat," offers something of a more folkloric horror story set in rural West Java. Though the dictatorship does not make an appearance in this story, it does offer an uncomfortable truth: that many people led normal lives, seemingly

---

[19] Figures regarding deaths under dictatorships are often quite difficult to get, but there is reason to believe this effort has proven especially difficult for assessors of the Suharto regime. The aforementioned massacre of communists was only one episode, committed from 1965-1966 as the Sukarno regime was ending. Other sporadic episodes of mass killings would occur, and there were of course more routine political killings carried out by the regime. Estimates of deaths under the Suharto regime have varied from hundreds of thousands to millions, but an exact figure will likely continue to prove allusive for scholars.

independent of the greater political machinations around them. The characters of this story certainly do not by any means experience a "normal" existence, and there *could* be reason to interpret the nightmarish goat-nurse as a representative of the dictatorship's violence. However, it seems more appropriate to say that the horror in this story is more rooted in a routine existence gone wrong during the Suharto dictatorship.

The General Fest whose legacy haunts the Hotel Armitage in "Endless Life" appears to be an amalgam of military strongmen. Bulkin establishes a compelling and informative biography for this general, including his parentage, brief information about his child and the town he grew up in.[20] The first two paragraphs of the story invoke Borges, who is well known for introducing elaborate history into his writing to inform a more realistic setting. The character of General Fest and his introduction can be compared to the introduction of Otto Dietrich zur Linde in Borges' "Deutsches Requiem:"

> "My name is Otto Dietrich zur Linde. One of my ancestors, Christoph zur Linde, died in the cavalry charge which decided the victory of Zorndorf. My maternal great-grandfather, Ulrich Forkel, was shot in the forests of Marchenoir by franc-tireurs, late in the year 1870…As for me, I will be executed as a torturer and a murderer. The tribunal acted justly; from the start I declared myself guilty."[21]

Zur Linde's introduction is information-laden. Borges references

---

[20] Nadia Bulkin, *She Said Destroy* (Petaluma: Word Horde, 2017).
[21] Jorge Luis Borges, *Labyrinths* (New York: Penguin, 2011), 173.

two very real European battles, but battles obscure enough to warrant reading the story alongside an encyclopedia. The introduction also includes a footnote, noting that zur Linde has not included his most well-known ancestor, a famous theologian.[22] This omission and the lack of zur Linde's guilt prove integral for the story, as he takes the Nazi ideology further than the sympathizers who Borges encountered in Buenos Aires. In this short time, Borges has made a whole character and populated his world.

Bulkin uses a similar technique in introducing General Fest:

> By the time of his death, Jon Henry was known as General Fest, or the Jackal, or-by foreign armies tasked with bringing him down-Black Ribbon, for the award he gave himself after he executed one hundred and five dissidents in a rebellious border province.[23]

The Jackal's introduction, like that of Zur Linde, is thick with history. Unlike Borges, Bulkin does not rely on real places and historical events for this story, but the events and places *seem* real because of the amount information provided. It avoids the "once upon a time" trap of fairy tales while still providing elements of fantasy, weaving them in matter-of-fact manner into what could otherwise be reality.

It is difficult, however, to suggest that Fest is merely an imagined Suharto. Such an impression would be a consequence of the reader bringing their own knowledge to the material, as Suharto is so effectively introduced at the start of the collection. Fest could just as

---

[22] Ibid.
[23] Nadia Bulkin, *She Said Destroy* (Petaluma: Word Horde, 2017).

easily be Kurtz or a more real military strongman such as Pinochet. For that matter, Fest could even be a colonizing general, perhaps Dutch. There is no shortage of dictators and generals for the reader to bring to their understanding of the man who was once Jon Henry. Certainly, the words "rebellious border province" invoke the history of Indonesia, particularly the annexation of East Timor. All of this stated, it is hard not to feel Suharto's shadow in this story.

But political violence has long been a subject in magical realism, with no greater example than magical realism's greatest masterpiece, *100 Years of Solitude*. No work has been as redefining and foundational to the genre than Gabriel García Márquez's long, sometimes sordid history of the Buendía family and the fictional town of Macondo. Márquez sets his story in the Thousand Days War, one of many conflicts between the Liberal and Conservative factions of Colombia. The Buendías are as affected by this violence as any citizens would be, despite how isolated Macondo is from the rest of Colombia. This is most true for one of the central characters of the novel, Colonel Aureliano Buendía.

The novel opens with a brief introduction of the Colonel:

> Many years later, as he faced the firing squad, Colonel Aureliano Buendía was to remember that distant afternoon when his father took him to discover ice.[24]

Aureliano Buendía's life is the most integral biography in *100 Years of Solitude*. It is also one of the most directly political threads in the book. Colonel Aureliano represents what many see as the tragic

---

[24] Gabriel Garcia Marquez, *One Hundred Years of Solitude* (New York: HarperCollins Publishers, 2006), 1.

and reoccurring political violence in Colombia, a figure who would be just at home in the Thousand Days War as he would be in La Violencia.[25] The Colonel begins his revolution out of a justified outrage but ends up becoming just as brutal as the conservatives he fights. Even after he retires back to Macondo to make golden fish, the Colonel is furious at the massacre of nearby workers by the United Fruit Company. Each of his three revolutions fail, and in the end the Colonel dies alone, not even to return as a ghost like his father Jose Arcadio Buendía.

100 Years of Solitude is peppered throughout with the reality of political violence, a reality that not even houses of ice and interceding ghosts can escape. Though the novel is an exploration of multi-causal phenomena, the actions of the Colonel is the greatest catalyst for the undoing of the Buendía family. His revolutionary ambition becomes bound up in a more consuming ambition of violence, and at the end of his career he becomes unrecognizable. His gift for prophecy fails him (a supernatural element which informs the novel's magical realism), as even knowledge of the future does not save him from the greater political structure around him; an eroding and corrosive environment which limits his choices and molds him into just another monster of war.

The Colonel is a more sympathetic monster than Fest, perhaps more sympathetic than Suharto, but a monster nonetheless. The use of his biography fleshes out the world of Macondo, populating it not only with the people he meets but the legacies of his actions as well. Streets are named after him, as are children. In this regard the Colonel

---

[25] "La Violencia" was a ten-year Civil War between liberals and conservatives, lasting from 1948 to 1958. The conflict was one of the bloodiest in the history of the country and was resolved only when Liberals and Conservatives agreed to share power through a rotating presidency.

feels just as real to Macondo as Suharto does to the characters in Bulkin's fiction. Buendía's wars and his exploits create a fictional history which is not all too distant from our world, and such proximity only makes the *realism* in magical realism that much stronger.

In this regard, Bulkin follows in the footsteps of many who came before her. The world, and its real violence, is part of a greater project to create a familiar setting where the unfamiliar can pass through. Her characters do not fall or crumble upon encountering the supernatural, but instead do their best to survive. Such a reaction is comparable to life with political violence, where horrible things may impose themselves into the lives of good, everyday people. Rarely do survivors of this phenomena have the luxury of crumbling, because to do so is to offer a moment of potentially lethal surrender. Like the last girl in Bulkin's "And When She Was Bad," they persist because they must.

But unlike Cortázar, Borges or Gabriel García Márquez, Bulkin's fiction is unapologetically horror. Treating a monster as if it is normal does not make a thing less monstrous, and the ghosts of her fiction do not stop being ghosts even though they do not rattle chains or drive people screaming from haunted houses. There is a horror in familiarity, in integrating the otherworldly into common experiences. Doing so only emphasizes the terrifying aspects of both.

Such is evident in "Live Through This," where Danielle Haas' ghost torments the town even though the boys who raped her go on to live normal lives. The horror of the story is not confined to Danielle's haunting, but the injustice of her experience as well. Danielle's story is an all too common one, the disappointing and terrible reality of many victims of sexual violence. There is a truth in her story, but not in her ghost. And in this truth lies the horror.

In this way, Bulkin represents both a departure from and a dialog with magical realism. While the horror in *100 Years of Solitude* is episodic, it is pervasive and omnipresent in the stories that compose *She Said Destroy*. While Bulkin's canvas may be similar to Macondo, her tones and narratives mark a territory of overlap between horror and magical realism; a fertile ground which has been hinted at since Borges dedicated his story "There Are More Things" to the memory of H. P. Lovecraft in 1975. To be sure, Bulkin is not the only writer who has combined magical realism and horror. Gwendolyn Kiste, Kurt Fawver and Thomas Ligotti all have veins of magical realism in their work. But magical realism pervades Bulkin's fiction, and her use of history (fictional and otherwise) marks her writing as distinct and ground-breaking.

Bibliography

Anderson, Benedict. *Imagined Communities: Reflections on the Origin and Spread of Nationalism.* New York: Verso Books, 2006.

Bitar, Sergio and Lowenthal, Abraham F., eds. *Democratic Transitions: Conversations with World Leaders.* Baltimore: John Hopkins University Press, 2015.

Borges, Jorge Luis. *Labyrinths: Selected Stories and Other Writings.* New York: Penguin, 2011.

Bowers, Maggie Ann. *Magic(al) Realism.* New York: Routledge: 2004.

Bulkin, Nadia. *She Said Destroy.* Petaluma: Word Horde, 2017.

Cortázar, Julio. *End of the Game and Other Stories.* New York: Harper Colophon Books, 1978.

Flores, Angel. "Magical Realism in Spanish American Fiction." *Hispania* vol. 38, no. 2, 1955. New York: Harper Colophon Books, 1978.

Marquez, Gabriel Garcia. *One Hundred Years of Solitude.* New York: HarperCollins Publishers, 2006.

Chronology of a Burn

By Tonya Liburd

MARCH 18, 11:12 a.m.

Suddenly something at the edge of Sarah's vision made her look over her shoulder, away from her computer to her stove, and she saw what was happening: a grease fire had erupted. She'd set the stove on high, getting ready to cook eggs, and she stared at the flames with disoriented, sleepy alarm. The first time this happened a few weeks ago she was able to blow on it to put the fire out. But this time in her haste to get the frying pan off the stove and blow, she spattered the oil onto her bare leg.

"Ow– oh, fuck..."

She felt the heat, but she was much more concerned about the oil that made it to the cupboard door where the white grocery bag full of trash hung. So, smoke gathered at the ceiling ominously from the burning garbage, spreading to other rooms. Grabbing the box of baking soda, she used it to put the flames out.

A combination of not being awake and alert and not mentally being all with it conspired to mar her mahogany skin with burns.

That body is mine, she remembered her mother telling her. *Until I say, that body is mine, and you don't have permission to mark up your skin.* Funny how something said slightly in jest in childhood could still mark your mentality, your approach to your body even as the years tumble by. She failed, once again, to keep her skin unblemished. She shared her mother's sentiment. Why mark up something beautiful?

Self-care was hard for her; she suffered from a mental illness, and she was on disability. She'd tried staying at a crisis center downtown that took people in for a few days, so she could get a handle on her morning meds routine again. But she was home now. Sometimes she stayed in bed past eleven a.m., sometimes till three p.m., a few times till even five. She'd also just lost a job, and the fact of it, the failure of it, weighed down on her, weighing her down into the bed, past her sheets... It was tough even to buy food, even when a $60-something check arrived to help things out.

March 22nd, 1:00 p.m.

The skin on the burns was thin, and the biggest patch cracked open, revealing white flesh, pores... white against the brown of the rest of her skin. It was tender to the touch.

March 25th, 4:00 p.m.

It was hard to keep the original skin covering the largest burn—an area almost the first half of her thumb—so Sarah let it come off. She figured it wouldn't be so bad since the wound would need to crust over and heal.

She decided against putting a band-aid strip on it. Even in Trinidad, the band-aid strips were peaches-and-cream colored. She'd never realized that band-aids were tailored towards a white person's skin tone till she came back to Canada in her teenage years.

Sarah settled down to read through the two hundred and forty stories for the literary review she helped run; it was a new magazine, and they didn't have first readers yet, but the submission response was high. They might have to publish it quarterly.

All the reading triggered her illness; the negative voices—intense, psychotic thoughts, really—came back: *It's too hard. You can't do this. Why do you think you can do this?*

She rubbed her temples and sighed.

You can do nothing.

You're doing nothing with your life.

She picked up the phone to call her good friend Elaine.

"Looks like I need to do a Cognitive Behavioral Therapy sheet," Sarah told her.

"That sounds prudent," Elaine agreed.

"Fucking negative voices. Feel like they're physical *things* in the back of my head. I'm having a hard time separating the distorted thinking from these negative voices, with how my life really is."

"It's all the reading you're pushing yourself to do right now, it's triggering things..."

"Yeah," Sarah said. "It's... getting bad."

"You can always ask for some time off."

Sarah shifted in her sheets at that, sitting on her bed. "Everyone agrees, though. This literary thing's helping me to get better and stay well. What else will I do with my life?"

"Hm. But take it easy, okay?"

"I will, I will; I overextended and now I'm paying for that. Do you have time?"

"Yup," her friend replied. "Get a sheet and off we go."

March 26th, 3:23 p.m.

There was a smaller burnt area, about the top segment of her pinky finger, going through the same process as the biggest one.

When Sarah confessed to her contact person at the mental health drop-in center that she hadn't gone to the walk-in-clinic—literally two minutes' walk from her apartment to get the burns checked out—they said, "Sarah... And the reason you haven't gone to the walk-in clinic yet is because?"

No reason. The same reason, always. As with millions of others, her mental illness made it hard to function, even to take fundamental care of herself.

The day after that, plasma and some crust formed.

Her friend April said she was getting concerned for Sarah and started calling her around eleven.

"For someone who gets up so late, you're remarkably hard to wake up," her friend said over the phone.

"I know. But I was worse a few weeks ago, remember? That's why I went to the crisis center... it'll take a couple weeks for my meds to kick in."

"That's true. I'll talk to you later in video chat?"

"Yup."

Sarah sighed; then, grunting under her breath, she lifted herself out of bed.

March 28th, 11:15 p.m.

One night, she took her meds a before she headed out, instead of when she came back from reading from her laptop at McDonald's. When the meds started to kick in, she was confused at first why she was feeling weird. Then she realized she was usually on the couch when this happened, so she would fade into sleep rather than feel woozy on her feet, being out and not snuggled up in her apartment. Swearing under her breath, and slightly concerned for her albeit brief walk home, she rose from her window seat to go. She bumped her leg against the edge of the table and felt some pain, then thought nothing more of it.

At home, however, in from the dark of night, she noticed a dark red stain on the deep blue of her jeans. She took them off to witness that the scab was completely gone. She saw an area on her skin that was shiny, and wet, bright reddish-fuchsia and still leaking some blood.

Now she would *really* have to go to the doctor, to the walk-in.

March 30th, 4:00 p.m.

She finally went to the walk-in clinic, but it was closing early. So, she had to muster up the energy to go the next day. Fortunately, she did. The doctor she saw was, in hindsight, careless—he put a whole wad of antibacterial ointment onto the burns and the smaller one, then put band aid strips over that. By the time she'd bought the ointment from the nearby pharmacy for her own home use and had gotten home, the band aids had fallen off. She went back down the stairs and found the other pair of band aid strips by the door to the stairs. Sighing, she tossed them into the bedroom garbage and put on new ones from her medicine cabinet.

The knowledge that being assertive was a process and that someday she'd not be so passive didn't comfort her. Her mind was excellent at waking up her emotions and realizations and outrage after the fact; what she'd like was for it to start *now*.

April 5th, 3:00 p.m.

She was afraid the same thing would happen again to the burn's scab, but it had been fine ever since she carefully, carefully took the sticky strips of band aid off, minding the edges where crust gathered. She even stopped going to McDonald's for a while just to make sure she would not re-injure it.

She was getting better.

She let her Case Manager—who assists in her managing self-care and independent living— know about the incident and the burns.

"Sarah, my dear... you have to stop putting things on high... cook at a lower temperature..."

Sarah sighed and nodded. And for a while she did nothing but that, making an effort to not go straight to the kitchen when she first woke up, to not leave the kitchen once the stove was on.

April 7th, 12:30 p.m.

The biggest burn began to itch occasionally.

When it's itching, that means it's healing, she remembered her mother would say.

Putting the crisply antiseptic-smelling, oily antibacterial ointment on the burn to mainly deal with the itch was proving to loosen the scab's edges. To eliminate accidental pulls by a stray passing hand, she got rid of the lifted edges, carefully peeling them off with her fingers. Eventually, one day, the remainder of the scab just lifted away upon examination while she was on a video chat. April on the other end was curious as to what the burn looked like now. Everyone she'd confided to about the injury seemed curious.

"Yep, that's a burn, all right, when you get to see how... pink it is," April said.

April 8th, 2:00 p.m.

Flaky.

That's how one could describe the surface of the largest burn now. The pink surface, spotted with developing brown pigmentation, was clear and flaky. When Sarah realized this, she momentarily wondered if it was started by the ointments or the lotions she put on it. But this was how the surface of the burn would be for the foreseeable future. She wondered how the burn's skin would be affected once the pigmentation spread from the preliminary dots and filled out the area. Would it be like the rest of her skin?

Sarah finally did something assertive. After consulting Elaine, she called her contact person at the mental health drop-in and requested he enquire to find out concretely why'd she lost her job; there was something Sarah felt she wasn't being told, and she said so. The contact person readily agreed and even said they could set up a meeting between the three of them. Her stomach tensing, she said no, they could talk to the person without her present.

Her contact said okay, and Sarah said goodbye.

After she hung up, she felt a weight lift off her shoulders. She wasn't used to having people be proactive about advocating for her. This was... quite a relief. She got a warm tingle deep in her gut, and it spread to a warm glow all over her skin. If she had an aura she'd imagine there was a soft, orangey-peach surrounding her now.

She'd get straight answers.

April 10th, 11:00 p.m.

The pigmentations within the largest burn were starting to meet, and if one didn't know how many brown spots there were at the beginning—ten—one would be confused.

The skin wasn't as flaky as before, but it was still dry - dry like the rest of her.

These days, she found herself rising before her friend called. The allure of eating her favorite, healthy cereals to make her rise was 50/50. But she wasn't risking staying in bed till three or five anymore.

Still, at nights, she could get depressed.

Nobody really likes or respects you.

One night, she tried reaching out to someone on her online friends' list. Someone she'd normally respect too much to risk revealing her issues. In their circles, this woman, a musician, was a big deal. Sarah still felt a bit intimidated and reverent when it came to deal with her. Sarah typed hi.

Prominent Musician: When am I going to meet you?

Sarah:- $$; yer in the States, I can't afford travelling, etc...

Sarah: I was feeling a bit depressed earlier; like 'nobody really likes/respects you'

Prominent Musician: That's the way most of us feel.

Prominent Musician: I like and respect you.

Sarah: Thanks. That means a lot.

Smiling slightly, Sarah sat back in her desk chair. *Reality:1. Distorted Thinking: 0.*

April 15th, 2:30 p.m.

Most of the small burns—burns from smaller drops, that had already shed and healed over—didn't need pigment spots and blended in with the rest of Sarah's skin, and only a slight shine from the scar tissue, when seen at a certain angle, made them stand out.

Sarah was getting up ahead of her friend's morning calls, and she'd been to the grocery store not once, but twice today. She was even thinking of perhaps going to watch a movie. She'd been out of the apartment the day before as well. It would seem her meds were beginning to kick in, and she'd done it without having to go to a hospital proper for a two-week stay, which is how long meds take to work if you've been off them.

She was, however, officially burnt out from reading. Others had said that she should give up the reading, that she may have taken on too much, and for several weeks she persisted until she had to admit her limits to herself. She was being given a break from the literary journal until she wasn't feeling her illness like a pressure in the back of her head.

It'd been a few days. She was on her way home, and as was her habit when taking public transit, she opened her phone to her Kindle to read along the way.

She stopped.

No overwhelming pressure in the back of her mind.

She smiled. This was a good sign. She was getting better.

Not whole, not cured—like a past therapist said, it's alright not to be perfect—but progressively better.

And okay.

The Blind Opera

By Sean M. Thompson

OVERTURE

THEY TIE you to a chair black as empty promises in the moonlight. Their lab coats are crisp, blinding white as newscaster-teeth as they inspect you with the cold gaze of birds of prey. You had been the kind of terrified where you only realized you were begging after the fact. As to what you articulated in your pleas, however many days earlier, you can't remember.

They'd thrown a black hood over your head, driven you for countless hours, to where you can only speculate: somewhere arid and remote based on the heat and lack of other sounds such as cars or planes. Fear grips you in a stranglehold, for in honesty what good has ever happened at a remote location in the middle of the desert?

You'd never met your kidnappers, but their black suits screamed government, CIA or NSA, some branch of intelligence. Knowing this fact does nothing to quell the terror as it lights up your body, surging through your blood like fast-acting poison.

When they finally remove the hood, your vision swims snow-blind. The time without direct light has made you like a subterranean creature daring to break the surface. You wonder if this is it, if this is how you die. You'd always assumed a heart attack, cancer, a stroke, one of the typical ailments to strike down the animal known as man in the declining years. Never in your strangest nightmares had you assumed a classified document would lead to a no doubt prolonged and agonizing murder at the hands of nameless operatives and scientists.

One man steps forward from amongst the procession of men in white coats like robes for some cult of government.

"It is a pleasure to meet you, sir. It's not every day we find a man who's been able to watch all six episodes before we track him down. It is exceedingly rare to find someone of your mental fortitude. Takes a strong constitution to view such awfulness."

"Please. I won't tell anyone anything."

"We know you won't. You won't be able to."

"I don't understand."

"Such is the nature of progress."

The scientist, in his wire-framed glasses, gives you the slightest hint of a smile, the corners of his mouth shifting almost imperceptibly. The bottom of your stomach falls out, your mind beginning to race.

"No. Oh, Please. Please, no-"

"Oh, come now. Stiff upper lip. This is, after all, what you've really longed for. To see the footage we captured. To truly experience the thing that makes the little show you've been so desperate to find so compelling! It is truly miraculous the varied responses we see. But you of course know this. You've watched all six episodes."

"You can't do this!"

The scientist leans in, the lenses of his glasses catching the overhead light shielding his eyes from view.

"We can do whatever we want. We have absolute authority from the government of the United States of America, son. If we really wanted to, we could torture you slow, claim it was for scientific purposes."

He turns from you, throws his hands in the air like an off-Broadway ham.

"By God, you could say that's what we're about to do!"

They exit the room, and the lights dim to nothing. A monitor drops from the ceiling into your sight line. The footage begins to play. As the shadows dance across the screen, you feel your sanity begin its slow unraveling.

RECITATIVE

The SUV turns the corner of the parking garage, overhead lights glinting off tinted windows. Cold steel smiles in the frozen Detroit night, while you sit in a comparatively tiny compact car, the heat up full blast as your fingers and feet burn with the cold. Extremities succumbing to winter, this ache in the bones screams for painkillers and rest, sensations you've grown to ignore, stubborn as you are. Mom always said you had to have things your way.

There's a man you must talk to, presumably in the enormous vehicle fast approaching, an informant who goes only by Scythe. Over the phone in your apartment, a voice heavily modulated, told you: *I've heard you want to know about* The Blind Opera. *I think I can be of some assistance.*

You're not a private investigator or film critic. A morbid curiosity and an isolated life lending itself to obsession are responsible for the location you find yourself within.

A lifelong devotee of cinema, of celluloid, of performance and theatrics, chiaroscuro lighting and Expressionist angles, you developed a fascination with independent films; the near budget-less attempts to transmogrify bad or out-of-practice actors and janky basement sets into visual art stronger than the sum of its parts. In short, you were looking for the true magic amongst the two-bit hacks. But soon you realized you had a very specific taste. You wanted the weird, the depraved, the desperate, and the damned. And like any drug addict, before long you had to up your fix.

The internet had become a valuable tool for millions of aspiring filmmakers, and technological advancement meant they could create as fast as the market could consume, albeit unsteadily in a market where monetary gain proved scant or nonexistent. These years have found you watching web series, shorts from amateurs and hacks, all manner of terrible drivel, in an effort to dig through the filth to find diamonds of terror and obscenity.

One day you found a message board in which a user named BirdDog666 wrote: *I saw a few episodes of this horror web series. It was called* The Blind Opera. *It was really weird, the first episode was this dude wandering around on the streets, falling in alleys, screaming to himself. The second episode was a woman sitting in a room with a single lamp on, scratching at her forearms. The practical effects were really solid, the wounds looked really convincing. I only got to watch two episodes before the hosting site took all six down.*

After that, you'd read all you could. Finding *The Blind Opera* became tantamount to finding the Holy Grail. This was what you'd been searching for, what you knew in your churning guts was the very essence of everything you longed for so dearly. Every waking minute outside of your office job you scoured the web for hints as to where the web series might be. You knew it wasn't gone entirely.

The SUV parks, engine idling, lying in wait for movement like some great, dark beast of metal. A large man with neck tattoos steps out in a business casual ensemble, all veins and muscles, beady brown eyes under a black wool hat. You're waiting for the informant to step out when you realize the large man is holding a plastic bag filled with a folder and a USB stick.

There were scatterings of people who'd seen the series well after its release date in June of 2015. Months would go by without any word, only to have a man in Texas post about seeing it at a friend's, or a woman in Massachusetts claiming to have seen a copy of it for sale from a drug dealer. A teenaged boy in Nebraska finding a copy on DVD in his dad's workshop. A librarian in Colorado seeing a very skinny twenty-something watching the third episode on one of the computers, and when asked to shut off the video, getting irate and trying to attack her with a knife. Blips like these all over the United States, mentions out of the country too.

"Money first."

You hand him the envelope, amazed at spending five grand to see what might be simply a rinky-dink web serial. But that itch, you must know, the perverse desire to see humanity at its worst, warped into a visual medium, into artistic expression; a pearl in the most mutated and deformed oyster.

Scythe hands over the plastic bag with the folder and USB stick. You turn to head back to your car when he puts a meaty hand on your shoulder.

"Do you know why I go by this name?"

"No," you say.

"I go by Scythe because I bring death."

He points to the bag in your hand. "That there is death sure as the worst cancer."

He turns, and his words root around in your brain, even as his vehicle peels off. You should be concerned, but you're so excited to finally see the series that the weight of his prophecy doesn't strain as much as it should.

Would that it had.

ARIA

The folder contains information you never would have expected. In a heavily redacted document you read about *Project Theia*. You have to search the Internet for the meaning of the word; turns out it's a Roman goddess of sight, a Titan. Cryptic black-ops bullshit.

From what you can gather, *Project Theia* was a classified experiment with a Hadron collider type device, nothing all that innovative in the search for new subatomic particles. The special thing about said project was that they were able to create a video camera capable of capturing the tiniest particles, capable of seeing things the naked human eye could not detect. To what end you're not intelligent enough to rightly say, though you assume something to do with research into how subatomic particles work.

The next page describes the team's shock when they discovered shapes in the footage they captured, shadows moving, and the language is intentionally vague and almost all the rest of the document is redacted.

The next document in the folder simply details the course of events leading to the creation of *The Blind Opera*. A pissed off scientist stole the video and sold it to a very rich man and avid science nerd. Said man fancied himself an avant-garde artist, a director of the experimental in the vein of Lynch or Bergman. With his tremendous wealth, said man, whose name is redacted in the document, set out to make his sadistic art. He'd gone to court for attempted murder and managed to walk away clean.

As if revolving around a stolen video from a classified government project wasn't enough reason for the web serial to be taken down swiftly, the document revealed that the last episode of the series, episode six, included a prominent senator.

This information only makes you all the hungrier to watch.

You insert the USB stick into your laptop, shut the Wi-Fi off, and open the folder labeled *TBO*. You click on the first episode, and the images flash across the screen. A man hacking off his own arm, screaming all the while. Had you not read the document, you'd applaud the effects and cinema verité. But now, of course, you know better, the bile rising in your throat.

RECITATIVE

You're wandering through the desert when you come out of the haze. Your hands are stained with blood, the plain grey t-shirt they provided you much the same. You're not sure how you escaped the lab, but a terrible suspicion percolates in your grey matter.

Up ahead you see a diner, neon lights shining on top: *Jill's*. A scattering of motorcycles in the parking lot, one big rig, and a rusted old Ford. Before you can second-guess walking in, you enter.

A bell above the door dings. A waitress on the tail end of thirty stands by the counter, staring off at nothing, makes eye contact. "Hey, honey. Sit anywhere you like."

She seems very nonchalant about the fact you're soaked in blood, but who knows? Maybe this happens every week.

"Can I use your bathroom?"

"Off on the left," she says, then walks over to a booth in the corner and talks to a customer, a tall woman with dirty blonde hair.

You clean your hands off in the sink, rinse out your shirt and hope it dries fast in the heat.

A glimpse of your face in the mirror makes you recoil. Dried, dark red spatter dots your cheeks. You scrub vigorously.

You grab a booth by the window, pleased to find your wallet with all its cards and cash still nestled inside.

"What can I get for you?"

"What state is this?"

"New Mexico."

"What…"

"I can give you some time."

"Coffee. Cream please."

"You got it."

You inspect the other patrons: guys with long hair and leather vests at the booth; a man in a blue trucker hat at a booth by the bathroom; the tall woman you'd clocked earlier at the opposite end in a booth; the waitress, a cook in the back. Not one of them seems alarmed at the state of you.

The waitress brings coffee, good and strong. She brings a glass of water. You order a tuna melt and some fries. All normal stuff, but an undercurrent seems to be rippling through the diner. You can't pin it down. The people seem normal, but the idea they could erupt into violence permeates the room like steam.

The waitress comes back. Her eyes go black.

"You see, but you can't see," she says.

You drop the mug of coffee, which shatters on the counter top. The waitress laughs.

"What is this?"

"You're behind, honey."

"Behind what?"

"The curtain. The metaphor is pretty nifty, ain't it? You exist but can't see. You go about thinking your lives are important, dramatic. But you never know you're just blind actors on a stage, feeling your way through the dark. Ain't that a kick in the walnuts?"

"I don't understand!"

Standing, you go to leave, and the woman at the booth lithely walks over to place a hand on your shoulder. Her eyes flicker black, then normalize.

"Cool your jets. You're to be commended. Only one has lasted as long as you, dude. The director."

A flash: every person in the diner dead, bullet holes riddling their corpses like sores, the smell of copper, gun smoke in the air. You stare at a trembling hand, the pistol still warm in the palm. There is a disconnect, and it takes you a few seconds to realize the hand is yours. The gun slips from your fingers, disappears before it hits the floor.

"What the hell is happening to me!"

You slump into the nearest booth, strength gone from your knees. Place your face in your hands, rocking back and forth from the strain.

"You're behind the curtain, brother. You see what lies behind," one of the guys in the leather vest says.

"I don't understand!"

"You're not capable of fully grasping, chief. This is easier. Most of you die within an hour, hour and a half. But you've managed to take the turns without turning into road pizza. So, right on."

Fingers twitch on your hands, spasms in your limbs. The diner full of dead souls stares on, eyes black as oil. You grind your teeth, jaw clenching. True forms materialize, the corpses now full of holes leaking fluid, essences draining away.

This is the cost of seeing the truth, the ramifications of what lies behind; achieving what the religious would call spiritual enlightenment: Nirvana, heaven, concepts presuming travel above or below. The answer is through, the answer is behind; unseen yet present, a higher plane merged within the existing; the concept of matter, yet denser, permeation. And even as you think this you have no idea when you acquired such knowledge.

"What do I do?"

"Don't ask me, honey," the waitress says. "I'm dead."

Her skin is tinged blue, bullet wounds in her throat, head, and chest. As quickly as these prophets rose from the dead to speak, now they're back in their final repose, where you shot them. It occurs to you then that you're a multiple murderer; this doesn't bother you nearly as much as it should, or perhaps you're in shock. The gun isn't anywhere you can see.

You dig through the pockets of the dead woman at the far booth, grab her keys, take cash from her wallet. Her rusty Ford awaits in the parking lot.

You sit in the Ford, planning your next move. You finally decide to drive east. Back to your apartment.

You need to find Scythe.

FINALE

The SUV sits in the driveway like a roadside attraction no one visits anymore, its finish caked white with salt. You feel like this car, stained and abandoned. Happiness, it seemed, was a sentiment invented by greeting card companies and made for TV movies, not an actual emotion experienced by the terrible conglomeration of twisted sinew and electrical impulses you are horrified to call your body.

You're not sure what you expected, but the large mansion looming ahead is very far from your fretful imaginings. Though it occurs to you that the informant and the rich man who bought the footage from *Project Theia* are the same person; the truth locks into place, you wonder how you hadn't put the pieces together sooner. You *were* being slowly tortured by the government... c'est la vie.

Informants were hard to predict by nature; as such you try to be as cautious as possible being in a fractured state of existence and with your sanity like a shattered vase glued clumsily back together. You park the stolen truck by a large marble statue of a lion, make your way to the front door. Sweat slicks your palm as you try the front door to find it unlocked. *Practically an invitation.*

A step through the door and vertigo hits you hard as a sledgehammer to the temple.

You place your hand on the marble balustrade: the surface slowly squishes like Jell-O. The hairs on your arms stand up as if a massive amount of static electricity were inside the mansion. Each step feels like walking through quicksand; your feet sink into the floor ever so slightly with each step.

At the top of the stairs, two hallways lead to the left and right.

You take the left-hand path. Flashes of images strobe in your mind as you approach an open doorway: your thumbs bursting through a scientist's eye socket as he screams; turning a machine gun on a guard outside the building; fleeing into the desert; and this very hallway, walking towards this very door. Shadows sway in your peripheral vision, a trick of the light, extreme stress, or perhaps dehydration and fatigue finally setting in.

Except you know better. You have been to places you can't return from unscathed.

Inside the room, Scythe reclines in an office chair, his feet on a desk made of what looks like volcanic rock. The big man's in jeans and a black tank top, tattoos prominent along his heavily muscled frame; the tattoo on his neck is finally clear now that its path isn't obscured by clothing: shadows like sheets on a clothesline blown to and fro by heavy wind, cascading down from neck to ribs.

"I've seen it, you know. I've traveled as you have."

Scythe motions to a chair opposite the desk, and you sit even while a memory ignites your mind's eye: the very same man before you, handing you a fancy digital video camera.

"You gave me a camera."

"No. But if you saw that, then I will."

"This doesn't make sense."

"And thus, you see the essential nature of reality and our place therein. Feels like a dream, right? A dream within a dream. Yet the way things are now is truer than the performances of so many years before, though these of course had their own merits and are not to be discredited. Do you know why I called it *The Blind Opera*?"

"The metaphor is 'pretty nifty'?"

"No."

"Then why?"

"How do you think you got out of that room? What hypothesis have you imagined?"

"I killed the scientists, then I killed the guards."

"Then how did you get off the base?"

"I..."

But you don't really know. All you remember is coming to in the desert, and then the diner.

"I don't know how I got to the diner."

"This reality is only a projection. In this way it's quite like cinema. When you see the true nature of reality, can see where the projection starts, you can learn to navigate around it, through it."

"Behind it."

"Yes."

The shadows, the way they swayed as you arrived, they stir thoughts, questions.

"How?"

"*How?* I don't presume to *really* understand how it works. To paraphrase the great Arthur C. Clarke: if science becomes complex enough it becomes indistinguishable from magic."

Memories of black ichor, trudging through the substance, feeling a sentience hinting at something far larger hidden behind dark shadows.

"Expertise requires many trips. For a novice you've got quite the knack. There are byways hidden behind crumbling towers, passageways to caves beneath the projection."

"Behind."

"However you wish to phrase it."

You hold your hand before your face; flesh lifts from the bones like dust in a vacuum.

"Jesus Christ."

"We shall be the new messiahs."

"Behind the curtain," you say, in a daze. The flesh of your arms ripples like lake water in a light breeze.

There's a strange comfort you feel, being in the room with this man. A kinship. You have survived a shared trauma, like soldiers. Anyone else you impart this secret knowledge to will never be the same. And, upon reflection, this is for the best. You don't tell children war stories unless you're grooming them.

"Come, friend. Let us travel the spaces between."

He takes your hand, and you exit his office, walking down a hall that is now endless, growing progressively darker with each step. The impression of shapes is about you, a sound you have trouble equating to anything you've known. The closest analogue is an enormous wind tunnel combined with the sound of a hull-breeched spacecraft; the indifferent, obsidian vacuum, that pull is the same as the one that acts upon you now. Your movement slows, a light source catching your eye; it's the parking garage from weeks ago. You see yourself, lock eyes with yourself, but if this past self notices he shows no indication. The scene comes apart, that's the best way you can think of it, shadows moving atom by atom; elongated spirals of dark matter, this is what you think while witnessing them. They are not just the absence of light, they are the inverse of life; they are the stagehands, and you and Scythe are now the directors.

A terrible cacophony of screams through liquid. There's an enormous black puddle, the semblance of many human faces within it. These faces are recognizable as the missing stars of the series.

Ahead, bright sunlight, and you've no way to measure the time it's taken to come upon this desert. The world shifts into the negative colors of camera film, and you see them, the shadows, like giant DNA helixes, looping and flying and crawling. They are everywhere and nowhere.

The cacti have roots of white lightning that lead into the heavens, the flowers on the ground and the rocks with the same brilliant white tendrils. This black light world blinks back to normal, though who can say which light is the true light now?

Ahead is a town, empty of citizens; a desolate landscape which seems to inform the old, warped wooden beams crookedly nailed together, the jagged signs with their faded paint monikers; Scythe motions to a crude building, an establishment no doubt grown unstable and indifferent. Marked in charcoal above the dilapidated batwing doors, in a malformed script, the word: *Theatre.*

Inside is the same black chair on which they strapped you, a man in a white lab coat now tied to the seat. A beam of sunlight shining through the window is a spotlight upon him.

"You should do the honors," Scythe says. He points to a projector above the black chair, set into the ceiling of the theatre.

You have seen the first season and know how to improve upon it. You extend your arm to point a finger at the projector; the device slowly lowers until it's at eye level with the screaming scientist.

He'll be a great actor for the first episode. With the work of two directors, two visionaries who now realize the punchline to the greatest joke of all time, there's no doubt that season two will be monumental.

Your mind drifts to scenes not yet filmed, actors giving the performances of a lifetime, wholly unaware. You and Scythe are set to become the greatest filmmakers in history.

Season two will be positively world ending.

Nightmares

By Désirée Zamorano

THE FIRST night all the children in the city dreamed of long and twisted dirt brown tentacles that reached out far from the depths under their beds and pulled at them, around their necks, around their torsos, binding their hands and feet. Each child, as they slept, felt these tentacles around their throats and knew that the goal of these skeletal limbs was to drag them down, deep into the earth, away from light and air. That night the adults dreamed of being a new born puppy, culled from its litter, and now fleeing, terrified, from a faceless, bodiless but omnipresent pursuer, who, they were convinced, wanted to skin them alive.

Bed partners or parents who weren't asleep, who were instead scrolling through a luminous field of text or reading with a small targeted light that Tuesday night, nudged their partner or gently prodded their charges awake, dispelling the miasma of the toxic nightmare.

All who slept through that night awoke to sweat-stained pajamas, fear and anxiety that had seeped and dampened the bedding.

The second night the adults and children dreamed of moths that covered their eyes, their ears, their nostrils and mouths with a fluttery lightness that gradually increased in pressure, those light wings gathering weight and mass as they pressed themselves against the dreamer and attempted to enter their body. Their bodies remained stiff and defenseless as moth wing powder passed into their noses, smeared against their unseeing eyes, the weight of hundreds, thousands of insects encircling, clustering, crushing, overwhelming, becoming an encapsulating cocoon; dreamers coughed and hacked as if choking, startling themselves awake.

Children and adults arose in the morning with long, drawn faces, ill-rested, anxious, barely registering the routines of the day that lay ahead, fearing the night that would follow.

The third night people and families fortified themselves with hot milk or hot cocoa or bottles of wine, bottles of liquor, or sleeping aids. Everyone knew you couldn't dream with a sleeping pill. The pills stopped the shrieking part of your brain, placating it, lulling it to silence.

Mind-numbing television, white noise, background music accompanied the soporifics and played in the background, in the bedroom, in the living room, in the den, all night long.

That night the city dreamed of sting rays and bat wings. Of deep silent oceans and brackish water. Of spindly jointed arms, like spider crabs, enveloping their bodies and dragging them down far away from light and air and day, until dim sunlight flattened against the windows.

The national media descended upon the city.

Local and national television, cable and radio news crews stood on the steps of the police station, of city hall, of the high schools, at the community college. Dozens of interviews were aired, while simultaneously highly credentialed sleeping disorder experts opined on the causes and implications of mass hysteria, mass shared delusion, and the complicated relationship between the populace and modern-day pressures and anxieties.

Health and nutrition experts offered their take on the flaws of the city's diet and exercise routine. Psychologists and psychiatrists offered, with cautious disclaimers, chiding pronouncements on how adult anxieties seep into the consciousness of children.

The fourth night was the worst, and no one would recount to one another what they had endured while sleeping. Certainly not the newscasters, whose own makeup needed additional layers of facial paint to hide what the dreams had uncovered within.

Experts, professionals and the media awaited the fifth night in a sort of excited anticipation. Saturday's places of worship addressed the city's crisis and offered their support and counseling.

The fifth night the city returned to its chaotic scattering of individual dreams and memories. People awoke, bleary with the surprise of a deep sleep, refreshed and eager to forget the previous nights' dreams.

Sunday's places of worship gave praise and thanks and cautionary tales.

The sixth night there were no dreams at all.

Monday morning the city's work week began with its citizenry refreshed, if not a little abashed. The national news crews drove off in search of more compelling stories; the local news covered the impending storm system. Schools and work places, homes and coffee shops, roads and walkways buzzed with the noises and conversations that had filled these spaces a week ago.

With a sigh of contented relief, the city closed its eyes on the seventh night.

At 3:17 in the morning, local city time, agencies from Tokyo to Newfoundland tracked bursts of seismic waves emanating from the city. Five hours later the state's energy companies, amid the turmoil and chaos, issued a statement asserting that they had never extracted oil or gas within hundreds of miles of the city.

The city itself no longer existed.

The houses, the apartments, the schools, the businesses, the offices, were no longer standing. There was not even rubble to mark where they had stood. An upheaval of fresh dirt covered five square miles, the ground where once had been a city. Surrounding pylons bent awkwardly downwards, trailing wires, tugging at the now taut lines of transmission towers that skimmed the dirt, as if these towers and wires were pulled with tremendous force from deep within the ground.

Far away from light and air and day.

The following evening across the state the children dreamed of long and twisted dirt brown tentacles that reached out far from the depths under their beds and pulled at them. The adults dreamed of being a new born puppy fleeing from a faceless, bodiless but omnipresent pursuer, who wanted to skin them alive.

"The Clown Puppet"—A Case Study

By Michael Cisco

N O ONE DOUBTS that Ligotti's work is weird fiction, but can we say how? What does it mean to categorize a story by genre? There are a number of questions that can help us approach an answer. Attempts to define genres often founder when they try to fix the genre's attributes, but how else can we think of genre? One approach would be to see genre, weird fiction in Ligotti's case, as something a story reproduces, instead of a category to which the story belongs. Each story has its own particular canon and reproduces its genre. Weird fiction does this by repeating and addressing certain concerns: Is reality stable? Is the supernatural a transcendent order? Is identity stable? Is there a bizarre event in the story? Is there a contrast between a bizarre aesthetic effect and the aesthetic conventions of fiction outside the genre? Does the story involve bizarre signs? Does the story involve an idea of destiny as self-aware? Now let's apply these questions to a story by Ligotti — "The Clown Puppet" — selected at random.

In this story, the unnamed narrator is working late one night at a "medicine shop" owned by a Mr. Vizniak when a puppet figure, whom the speaker has seen numerous times before, appears to him and then, presumably, absconds with Mr. Vizniak. The speaker is an auditory witness to the disappearance; Mr. Vizniak seems to recognize the puppet and is withdrawn from existence in much the way a marionette on stage is pulled up out of sight by its strings.

The story's canon brings together Lovecraft, M.R. James, and Hoffmann; all prominent writers of weird fiction. Ligotti introduces into this combination the style of Thomas Bernhard, whose work is not weird fiction. The story is written largely in a version of Bernhard's style, turned toward the purposes of weird fiction. From Lovecraft, he takes some aspects of setting — the derelict town — but more importantly, he takes a certain problem involving cosmic indifference. Ligotti once told me that his favorite story by M.R. James was "The Story of a Disappearance and an Appearance," which revolves around a Punch and Judy show. The puppet imagery in "The Clown Puppet" connects to this imagery, and the title of the James story could also just as readily be applied to this one. Finally, Hoffmann provides us with the figure of Mr. Vizniak, who seems to be a demoralized version of one of Hoffmann's adept characters, such as Counselor Krespel; from Hoffmann as well come the significance of gestures and even a kind of dancing in the story. "The Clown Puppet" reproduces the genre of weird fiction by combining these elements in the service of a new story, involving a new kind of narration.

Reality is presented in the story as unstable, in that it is at once an illusion and yet something that no amount of disillusionment can escape. That is, it is a dream without a waking "real" life to compare itself to. The supernatural element in the story would be the visit by the puppet; that this is not a hallucination is clear, because Mr. Vizniak also sees the red-gold light that heralds the visit, and the question of hallucination is productively undermined by the more sinister implication that the visit is anomalous only insofar as it is not really anomalous — more on this later. The supernatural in the story does reflect a transcendent order, but Ligotti escapes the reassurance that normally is associated with the idea of such an order by insisting that it is empty, or "nonsense." To put it another way, there is sense, but not for us. The only sense is that there is no sense. Sense is only an illusion. Identity seems to work in the same way, and, as is often the case, the sense of life and the world is regarded as the pillar of identity, so that an attack on the former likewise undermines the latter. There is plainly a bizarre event — the visit — although this is less an anomaly in contrast to normal everyday events, considering how generally low-key dreamlike the story is, and more a contrast between this visit and previous ones. There is a contrast between a bizarre aesthetic effect and the conventional expectations of a story; this is a weird tale in which the harbinger of doom comes not for the narrator but for someone else. The main aesthetic effect, however, is the very atypical division between horror, which is present in the story, and fear, which only affects Mr. Vizniak. The speaker, on the other hand, is not afraid, but outraged, and that outrage is the story's chief emotional affect. The bizarre event is manifestly a sign; the puppet is an emissary, operated by strings. Is there anyone or anything pulling the strings? Finally, destiny appears as something self-aware in the story insofar as the narrator is complicit with the story. We are told that, as far as he knows, he will receive only one visit in any given location. After each visit, he changes his location, without any apparent compulsion to do so. If he did not change locations, then there would be no further visits, so his evidently voluntary relocations seem to be intended to ensure that the visits continue. This suggests that the narrator is involved in the events of the story in the same elusive way that the dreamer is with the origin of the dream. This must be the case, because the dream must not come from outside the dreamer. If it did, then the story would lose efficacy. It would become the story of someone oppressed by a curse imposed from outside, which would then have to be explained if the story were to be satisfactory as a story, but that is not what this story is. Instead, the dream must involve the dreamer so that his identity itself is undermined. The victim of an inimical force is neatly defined as an individual by persecution, and this is not what is happening here. What we are to fear is not some random encounter with a malicious curse, but our own intangible reality as selves.

Reading the story more closely, we begin with the title, which situates the story at the intersection of one set of weird tales involving human effigies and another set that involves clowns, although a clown may be defined as a kind of human effigy. The first line remodels opening sentences like Lovecraft's "Life is a hideous thing" (from "Arthur Jermyn") and Poe's "Misery is manifold" (from "Berenice"). It is the statement of a philosophical thesis that the events of the story will bear out. Here we can appreciate the cumulative effect of the consistency of a writer like Ligotti, in that anyone familiar with his work will, on reading these words, suspect that it's the clown puppet speaking them, and even if it isn't, whoever is speaking them will turn out to be no different from a clown puppet (that is, a helpless mockery of a free human being). The first line states that the speaker is outraged by the failure of existence to make sense, or perhaps by the mocking appearance of sense existence presents, as if existence were real only insofar as it tricked you into believing it was real. Lovecraft worked up a parallel double-bind: the monstrous gods who personify the impersonality of the cosmos, who are indifferent to mankind, but not completely. They seem to want to humiliate mankind by "rubbing it in," but then that means they aren't indifferent to mankind.

Thomas Bernhard, the Austrian writer, developed a unique prose style involving the repetition of phrases with minor modifications. Bernhard's repetition has a way of sustaining focus on an idea while turning it, so to speak, this way and that, making it a kind of rhetorical sculpture that can be examined from a number of different sides. This gives us an affect too of precision and insistence. It looks the same no matter what your point of view is. Therefore, it is the way it looks.

The speaker adopts a position that is completely superior to reality, indicting it as a fraud, but not in the name of any superior sense; the speaker has no superior idea of reality, but *is* a superior reality. Reality fails to live up to him, to his standard of sense, and while the speaker can adopt any distance, from intimate to remote, the speaker is free, at least at this point, to survey all possible points of view. The narrator speaks as the embodiment of reality itself. As the narrative begins, it remains to be seen whether that freedom of movement in perspective will endure or whether the speaker will be beguiled again and become fixed. This is the conflict of the story, and the danger comes in the form of the visits.

The visits are bizarre signs. In this case, they are a volatile mixture of banality and the ironically self-aware employment of carefully selected tropes from weird fiction, like Mr. Vizniak, the man with the slightly fantastic, exotic name, who seems to bring an aura of strangeness into the ordinary with him, and the mysterious shop, which brings strangeness into the domain of business. The shop isn't a drug store or a pharmacy; it's a "medicine store." This is a very deft and elegant way to create a dreamlike sense around the story — simply refer to things by off-names. The shop only minimally qualifies as a shop, since it is situated in an out of the way place and it is very small. Mr. Vizniak lives above it, and so that conserves the footprint of the bizarre in an urban setting whose ordinariness can be assumed insofar as it is not really described in any detail: two weird spots, a shop and a home in two different locations, would already go too far toward making the city or town itself fantastical, and so the contrast would be weakened. Mr. Vizniak doesn't care if the shop is illuminated at night, or even if it is open or closed. This implies that the shop fulfills its purpose simply by being there, and this is entirely at odds with the logic of any commercial enterprise. Businesses grow, they don't try to remain as small as possible. It appears Mr. Vizniak has hired the narrator only for his own benefit, to distract him from his nonsense, not with sense, but with absence. The store doesn't make sense as a store. The peculiar sympathy between the speaker and Mr. Vizniak suggests, if not that they are the same person, something perhaps more radical, in that their being different persons amounts to no real difference. Continuity has already told us that Mr. Vizniak is one of Ligotti's Hoffmannlike agents of empty revelations, so his "special knowledge" is likely the truth of the story. He is an agent of the fictionalness of the story, and he knows it, or will realize it. The point here is that Ligotti is comparing the life you live right now with the tenuous, obviously phony existence of characters in stories, characters who aren't even especially plausible as characters. That, by means of a brilliant artistic turn, becomes the verisimilitude of the characters — they resemble us in their unrealness.

Across the street, there is "the meat store" — not a butcher shop. Just like the medicine store, this place has a willfully cruder name that is reinforced by the simple illuminated nouns that are among the only lights in the scene. This might have less to do with any notion that human life is just merely physical and fleshly and more to do with the idea that this deliberate crudeness makes the scene more plausibly physical by drawing our attention to the unreality of even our physical experience of life. Both the stores have something to do with death; "death nonsense" is the "worst" perhaps because with death there is strictly nothing to speak about at all. The freer we are to speak about something, that is, the more unconstrained we are by that thing, the more nonsensical what we say about it will be. So, if we maintain that the absence of life is the least of what we can experience, then perhaps we are least constrained when we discuss it, and so anything we say is extravagant. Ligotti's style is extravagantly anti-extravagant, that's how he has his cake and eats it too. That's part of the unique pleasure of reading him. So, we have a medicine shop, a meat shop, a medicine room, a toilet, and only in the toilet is there an opportunity for a character who cannot abide nonsense to collect himself. This seems like an evacuative, self-derogatory comment, although all these places involve bodies. I collect myself in the shitter. So, what does that make me?

The visit is so nonsensical that it makes the nonsensicality of reality obvious, which is why the speaker seems to privilege it. The visitor cheats so outrageously that the puppet's deception acts as a revelation instead. Each visit prompts a departure that only appears to be a change; changing locations, setting, personnel, all the elements of a real scene, but without the effect of actual change, and this reinforces the idea that everywhere the speaker only confronts the same seamlessly joined lying essence, one from which he vainly distinguishes himself. The figure appears without any physical mechanism, but this probably has less to do with the traditional difficulty in distinguishing between actual events and hallucinations that we find in a great deal of weird fiction and more to do with establishing the illusory nature of actual events. The sound the puppet makes, which corresponds with its transit across his field of vision, causes its appearance to be addressed to the speaker, since it seems to be interacting with his field of vision. The puppet's fixed expression gives us the problem: that the indifference and senselessness of reality does not strike human beings as mere neutrality but as a deliberate callousness, as if sense and care were not nonexistent but deliberately withheld from mankind and therefore possible. This is the most Lovecraftian element of this story. The odd digression about motions seems to be included in part to reinforce the idea of action without actor, or of events without being, or of reality being a performance — the quotation may be invented. It introduces a tone of parochial narrowness into the story which seems to contrast with the nihilism of the speaker. There is no alarm; the explanation is matter-of-fact, so we see this isn't about fear but about horror without fear. The puppet is nightmarish, but the speaker is indifferent. So where is the indifference? In the cosmos, or in the speaker?

The speaker is called upon to go through the motions of his own activity, here being a counterman at a drugstore, and so we can see this is why the visits are always associated with the performance of a specific duty rather than home visits. The motions you go through in a simple job are stereotyped and impersonal in a way that domestic activity, while perhaps just as mechanical and/or arbitrary, is personal. The self-awareness of the story emerges mainly in irony: the puppet is an effigy, so it has no proper identification. The closest thing it has to an identity would be the identity of the one who pulls the strings, but there is no indication that any such being exists.

Finally, emotion occurs, but it is anxiety and something like anger rather than fear. By presenting Mr. Vizniak's passport, however distorted, the puppet seems to be claiming to own the store, to be the speaker's employer, so this suggests a kind of endgame, that the truth is about to come out, that everything is a farce, and this is when the speaker becomes angry, and when Ligotti chooses to introduce Mr. Vizniak. He enters as the puppet leaves, and it becomes apparent that the medicine store should be visualized as a Punch-and-Judy style puppet booth, with characters coming and going as they do on stage, from left to right, disappearing behind curtains. This puts the speaker in the position of either the puppeteer or the audience. Mr. Vizniak hears sounds in his room above, and the puppet seems to have descended the stairs to enter the store, so this makes his room into something like the upper regions of a puppet stage where the puppets are stored. Mr. Vizniak beckons with a hand motion, like the puppet, and the speaker is primarily struck by the idea that another person is unprecedentedly entering into one of his visits — but is Mr. Vizniak another person? That the puppet should identify itself as Mr. Vizniak and then vanish as he appears suggests they are not different. It seems we are being prepared for the revelation of Mr. Vizniak as the puppet or puppet master. This is another way in which the story participates in the genre of weird fiction, by playing off expectations of this kind.

The speaker addresses his employer, but not as an employee. He speaks to Mr. Vizniak as if they were related. In a dreamlike touch, Mr. Vizniak seems to be coming into the shop from his bed, since he is not dressed for the street, but he enters from the street. The narrator tells him to go back to bed, presumably so that he will not encounter the puppet. This is one of the few acts by the speaker that reflect any volition at all. Is this because he wishes to protect Mr. Vizniak, or is it because he wants the visits to be his alone? Given the implications of the story so far, an encounter between Mr. Vizniak and the puppet would most likely result in the collapse of reality around the speaker, a final confirmation of nothingness, which his constant relocation after each visit seems intended to fend off. However, the speaker does not try vigorously to prevent Mr. Vizniak from entering the store. His resistance is not pronounced or intense; he seems to be weighed down by an overpowering, existential fatigue. It may be that he is getting tired of the farce or of his part in the play. On the other hand, Mr. Vizniak is genuinely afraid. Does his secret knowledge extend to his own unreality as a character in a story? His face is like a mask, his eyes are bright with fear. The puppet fulfills much the same function as a harbinger of death, but its appearance doesn't really herald death. Death is also nonsense. Perhaps this is something to do with the "meat store." The puppet is harbinger of the unreality of life, and, hence, also of death. This is the problem here for Ligotti aesthetically, infusing intensity into a deflating experience. How can there be any sense of danger involving a being whose existence is false? By being neutral and inert, the narrator is better able to blend with the reader to vicariously threaten the reader's own complacent sense of being real.

Mr. Vizniak sees the strange light, which confirms that the visit is not an experience for the speaker only. He speaks tonelessly; this detail, with the prior reference to a mask, augments the sense of impersonality around him. It seems he is losing concrete particularity. He retraces the steps of the puppet and the repetition of the verb "brushed" to describe the sound of his footsteps after he used the word himself to describe the sound of what was presumably the puppet going down the stairs, connects the two. Reading this, the genre reader begins to anticipate a climactic explosion of some kind coming from the rear of the shop. Perhaps the horrifying climax is the realization that there is nothing special about being visited, that those who see the nonsense for what it is are in the privileged position of being in on the joke, as opposed to the ignorant masses. Once offstage, Mr. Vizniak is whisked away like a puppet being yanked up out of sight on its strings; the foreboding this story creates then has to do with the supposition that we are all dangling from strings that are not only being jerked around, but can be yanked, pulling us into oblivion in a way that only suggests a reason or a destiny, but which might as readily be purely senseless.

Ligotti clearly and directly homes in on the instability of reality in this story, without any detour through a plausible landscape. The concentrated force of the story would be dissipated if there were any carefully-assembled real events to be undermined later by the arrival of the puppet; that plausible reality would be conjured only to be subverted anyway. This story comes from a place where it is no longer possible or worthwhile to conjure up a plausible reality to undermine. This is one of Ligotti's key innovations in weird fiction; he begins with the unreal and unwraps it within itself. The effect of this is to treat plausible reality as something already so blatantly compromised that it is no longer possible to create a passable facsimile of it in a story. It isn't necessary — and it may not be possible — to create the house of cards you intend to knock down. By starting with the unreal, Ligotti turns what is often in weird fiction an all-or-nothing, binary distinction between real and unreal into a continuum of escalating unreality. This affords creative room to explore unreality without having to invest in a version or idea of reality that is no longer viable. Having done this, Ligotti then can achieve bizarre effects by amplifying banality, so that the shocking discovery we have come to expect as genre readers is the unveiling of the ordinary as just the ordinary.

Part of the problem with artistic depictions of unreal experiences is that they are easily subsumed under one or another category, such as the hallucination or the supernatural. The event here is supernatural in that it is plainly not some technological trickery or neurological snafu; the speaker doesn't have the psychological intricacies of a Poe narrator or the traumas of a Hoffmann character, so it doesn't stand to reason that the visits would arise out of his weird mental state. Ligotti's supernatural does have a philosophical consistency in its nihilism; it may be that the emptiness of his supernatural compensates for its logic. The puppet is no surprise, not to anyone who encounters it, except insofar as it is strange for a nonsense cosmos to send an emissary to someone to announce that it is nonsense. The puppet is not bringing about an apocalypse or a prophetic judgement; its arrival is more like the realization of a truth that no one has the strength to deny any longer. The concept of nothing is still something, and so we must distinguish between the concept of nothing and the absence of being. To the extent that nothingness can be treated as something other than an identity, Ligotti unmakes identity. Ligotti's identities, in this story and elsewhere, do exist insofar as they must in order to realize they are illusory. This may be why the speaker has an ordinary attitude toward bizarre things. The closed, normal world turns out never to have been normal or closed, although Ligotti's vision is always closed, so in a way he weaponizes that idea of the world being closed; he doesn't open the closed world, he shows that the world is completely closed. This is another important innovation on his part: in this and other stories, largely by virtue of his exquisitely crafted tone of perfectionistic resignation, the revelation of a destiny always takes a closed form.

Nightly Senses

By Emmie Bristow

a lizard ran its way around
my light fixture. I swear.
the pattering *ttttt* woke me

and my tea ticks after I've
poured it from the kettle (screaming
        of course). but when I stick
my face in the steam it stops

I think my fridge ticks, too—
did that candle move? I thought
I set them exactly parallel
each base lined up, one slightly
taller than the other

I swear I hear memories
around me, faintly humming
old advertisements
eight hundred five eight eight
two three hundred, Empire! Today
(I always hear the cartoon smile after
that, the satisfying boom
                 of a commercial end, leaving
                 walls quiet again)
the living room goes dark
I picture a darker
figure splayed in the corner.
sometimes I hear him breathing
sometimes I feel his breath humid
against my exposed neck
his smile crackles

and sometimes I see my bedroom knob jiggle
up down up down
up down up down
and a black shadow swoops in
then out
before I can see him
 or ask his name
I'm paralyzed
sometimes I laugh
sometimes I cry
 both are uncontrollable, both real
 booming against the boxelder bug
ceilings. I picture them falling
 landing in my hair, laying eggs
 buried in my scalp and I itch

them out but they keep crawling
 into my crevices, into my darkness
I hear the candles moving, I swear.
 where is that lizard? it needs to eat these bugs
I think the kettle's screaming again
 I need to take care of it
 let its steam cloud my face

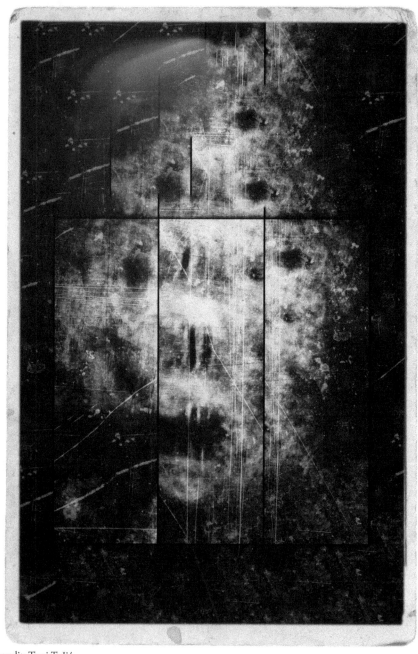

credit: Toni Tošić

The Nightmare Man

By L'Erin Ogle

T HE NIGHTMARE MAN comes all suction cup mouths and spider fingers.

The door hisses on the carpet, and he slithers in. Pull the covers up over your head and whisper this mantra. It's just a dream, it's just a dream, it's just a dream.

We eat breakfast alone on weekdays. mom has to be at work in the city by 8 am, but it takes her an hour to get there during rush hour. She wakes us up and makes us get out of bed. Otherwise we might oversleep and miss the bus, and there's no one to give us a ride. Sometimes it's hard to leave the bed if the Nightmare Man has come.

He was here last night. I know before I see Julie's purple crescent moons. It's written in dirty chalk smudges under her eyes.

We've moved twice since the Nightmare Man started coming. He still finds us.

Not because of him. Just one cheap rental to the next, rust circles in the toilets and bathtubs. We're not allowed to talk about the Nightmare Man.

I pick at the table instead of eating, peel strips of old finish away. My cereal expands with milk, turns into mush. Julie zombie stares into space.

We wait for the bus at the end of the driveway. Gray slush covers the ground, and I look for footprints, but the Nightmare Man didn't leave any. He never does.

Julie is crying silently, and I lace my fingers with hers. "It was just a bad dream," I tell her.

"I know," she says without making a sound.

The Nightmare Man came five years ago, two days after Julie turned twelve. I found her crying, eyes red, body shaking. Mom had her arm around her, which was odd. We weren't big on touching. I can count the number of times she or daddy hugged me. Seven times, if you count the one-armed kind.

"It's fine," mom said, snapping at me. "Julie just had a bad dream."

Julie didn't look up. The tension wound around and made it hard to breathe, and I sidled back in my room. It was the best thing to pretend we didn't exist at home. The less we were noticed, the happier they seemed.

They didn't hit us or anything like that. They just didn't want to be bothered. I had trouble learning somersaults as a kid, and Julie coached me through it, and I tugged my mom's pants to show her I had finally got it.

"Jesus Christ, what now?" she asked. "Can't I get five fucking minutes away from you?"

"Wh-what happened?" I asked Julie, later, on the bus. I stuttered back then, too. I understood it was hard on mom. Dad was always working, and she had to work and cook and clean and go to conferences, plus take me to "my goddamn worthless" speech therapy.

"It was just a dream," she said, and tucked her hair in her mouth, sucked the ends. I'd never seen her do that before.

"About what?"

"A bad man," she replied. "He had long arms and long legs, and he was all shadows and a sucker mouth."

"A sucker mouth?"

"Yeah," she said. Julie's hair fell from her lips. "He came into my room. He pulled the blankets off me. He stared at me for a long time. Then he breathed on me."

"He buh-buh- "

"Yes, he breathed on me." Julie finished my sentences all the time even when I didn't stutter. She didn't like to wait on me.

"Were you scared?"

"Obviously, retard," she said, turning away, her forehead on the window.

She never called me retard. Kids at school did. I tried, did all the things I was supposed to. Took a deep breath. Organized my thoughts. Spoke slowly and pictured the words leaving my lips. Tried to have backup words ready, but my stammer always came out to carry the words away and leave me red faced and airless, chest on fire.

"You're not retarded," my speech therapist told me. "You just have a couple of crossed wires. You've got all these thoughts in your brain, and things get a little caught up in the big tangle of ideas you've got. You're probably smarter than me, actually."

Julie thought that too.

So, when Julie called me a retard, I knew she didn't mean it. My sister saved me. She always sat with me. She could have been popular, being pretty, but I was the anchor that pulled her back down to Loserville. She would never had called me a retard unless she needed me to leave it alone.

I can't leave things alone, mom says. Like a goddamn puppy with a stick, gnawing it to bits.

Julie and I didn't talk about the Nightmare Man again.

We sit together on the bus, second seat, behind the driver. When we get on, Raymond says, "It's the sleazy sisters!" Lots of things rhyme with Beasley, but sleazy stuck with us through middle school into high school. Julie puts her hair in her mouth, pulling it across her face in a silk curtain.

"Do us a favor and pop those craters on your face, Zitman," Clay says from the back of the bus, and people laugh. Clay never called me retard back in grade school. I remembered who didn't more than who did.

"Go fuck yourself, Gumby," Raymond replies. I like Clay, but his arms and legs are long and slender, like the Nightmare Man's. I can see them turning to tentacles, all sucker mouths at the end. It makes me so sick I can't look at him. He sits next to me in Algebra (the dumb algebra, for kids like me that don't get numbers and letters mixing). My mind gets all jumbled up with those, too. When Clay talks to me, I stare at the print in my textbook until it blurs.

"Autistic?" Mom said, at a parent teacher conference. "You people and your fancy words. She ain't autistic. She's spoiled, she's just gotta focus."

That's what she told me all the time. Focus, goddammit. But things moved around on me. Or I missed them. I could be looking for something and staring right at it, and I wouldn't see it. Crossed wires. Jumbled up head.

"Hey, Daisy," Clay says today. "What up?"

"Nothing," I mumble. I have a scar on my knuckle where I bit it last year to keep quiet, so the Nightmare Man didn't know I was there, under the sheets. It didn't work.

It never works.

"Yeah, me neither," he replies.

I sneak a look at him, slouching in his chair, his fingers sliding over the screen. He has dark hair and a big mouth full of white teeth.

I am missing a molar. It got a bad cavity and rotted away. Too much sugar, the dentist said. Floss and brush every day. I do, because we don't have money to go the dentist. I only got to go because the cancer hadn't rotted granny's yet. She had money, but we never did. Mom didn't like her mom. "Goddamn cheap bitch," she said all the time. "Why is she holding onto her damn money? You can't take it with you."

But the money was imaginary. When granny died, the hospice and the medical bills had eaten every penny. We cremated her, cause it was cheap. Now we buy big bags of generic cereal with second thought names and dollar freezer meals. We get free lunch, and Julie doesn't eat, she doesn't want to stand in line and have to say her name loud over the other kids, have everyone know she's on the list.

Every day is exactly the same here.

We split the lunch I get. Julie eats all the potatoes, but I don't complain. She feels empty today. It's the kind of empty that yawns inside, and all the potatoes in the world can't fill it, but it's something to do.

I eat the meat loaf and push it around the space where my molar used to be.

"We should kill him," Julie says.

"Who?"

"You know," she says.

I push more food around in my mouth. I try to identify a taste, but it has none, so I pour salt on it. Not pepper. Pepper flakes make me think of ants, the relentless pursuit of crumbs and leftovers. Scurrying around, swarming things.

"How?" I say finally.

"We hide a knife in our bed. The next time he comes, we stab him."

In our dreams, we scream. They stop at our vocal cords. Nothing comes out.

Because it's just a dream.

"It's just a bad dream," I say.

Julie puts the spoon down. "Is it?"

I don't know.

We're not allowed to talk about the Nightmare Man.

I told granny about him before she died. She was still smoking, her oxygen tank turned off, and the tubing looped around it. She had a Pall Mall between her lips, and her eyes were slitted at me through the smoke.

"The Nightmare Man?" Granny dropped a run of spades down, slapped her discard down. In my head, I said a goddamn two. Granny talked like Mom but better. I mostly talk to myself in her voice. "What the hell's a Nightmare Man?"

"He comes in your dreams." I pick up the two of diamonds anyway, because I have the ace, and discard the nine of hearts. "He's got long arms and legs, like an octopus. They have spider fingers on the end that pinch. And a sucker mouth."

"A sucker mouth? What in the hell is that?"

"Like one of those big fish at the bottom of fish tanks. They suck everything up. Sucker mouth."

"Yeah?" Granny said. Her eyes were dulled behind the lids, but the old sharpness peered out at me. "You and Julie both see him?"

"Yeah. Sometimes we even get hurt in our dreams," I told her.

"Huh," she said. Three letters but something more. You could see her mind trying to work past the haze of pain pills. She dragged on her cigarette. She didn't ask more questions. She looked at me funny a couple times, like she wanted to say something, but she didn't.

Julie hides one of the big kitchen knives in her pillowcase. It doesn't have a cover, and I worry she'll cut her face, but she says she'll be careful. We don't talk about it after that.

A week passes, no Nightmare Man. The slush melts, and this

kid Ben begins sitting with us at lunch. He has long hair and wears all black, paints his nails black and everything. He talks about music every minute he isn't eating. He buys sodas and chips and we share them, even me.

Julie has friends, wins them with her sharp eyes and blond hair. She talks to Ben more than she's ever talked in her life. She talks about how she hates this town, hates mom, school, basically everything. She doesn't talk about the Nightmare Man. She wants to go a beach somewhere, she says to Ben. Lie on the sand, make sand angels, swim in the ocean.

"You'd look good in a bikini," Ben says. He has eyes that shine when he looks at her.

I ride the bus home alone, now. I don't have any friends. But it's ok. I like to watch people. I think everyone has their little secrets all divided up into different places. If you watch real close, you can see the real feelings behind why they say and do stuff. Like Raymond, he always hitches his pants up and sucks his gut in. When he eats, he hides what he's eating in his hand. He always tugs his shirt down, and he rolls his back so he looks smaller. He's mean because he doesn't like himself. If you understand people, it's a lot harder to be mad at them.

Julie rides home with Ben every day. I press my forehead against the glass like she used to and watch the houses go by. I bet they all have their own nightmares inside.

Saturday morning, Julie won't get up. I go into her bedroom, and the dark smudges are back. Lots of moons, purple curves, dot her collarbone. She pulls the comforter up to her chin.

"Go away," she says.

"Why didn't you stab him?" I whisper, looking at the door. "Where's the knife?"

A tear comes to the rim of her eyelid, hovers. "I couldn't," she says. The tear jumps and tracks down her cheek.

"Why?"

"I couldn't," she whispers.

We used to go to granny's every weekend. She smoked unfiltered cigarettes and her fridge was stuffed with cans of Diet Pepsi. We played gin rummy and War with her, and she took us the library, where we checked out books.

Julie didn't read hers, but I did. I read *A Wrinkle in Time* seventeen times. I read *She's Come Undone* and I read *The Perks of Being a Wallflower*, and sometimes I would cry so hard the paper wrinkled with it. Certain scenes bubbled up in my throat and got stuck, and I felt all the things I felt like razors cutting me up inside. Stop hurting them, I'd want to say to the bad characters in the book. I could feel all that pain, through pages, cutting through the mess in my mind.

Granny was more home than I ever had, in her kitchen with the dog salt and pepper shakers and smoky haze, and I wish Granny would have taken us away. But the cancer came and whittled her away.

"What were you thinking?" mom shouted. She had been on the phone with granny, hissing things real mean like across the receiver.

"Telling your grandma about some stupid dreams? The cancer's goddamn eating her up, and you fill her head with that bullshit? What the hell's the matter with you?"

She slapped me, the only time she ever hit me. It landed on the back of my head and shook my teeth. I bit my tongue so I wouldn't cry.

"You want your granny's last days here to be worrying about some dumb nightmare? You want her to die afraid? You know, I don't think I ought to let you go back there, Daisy."

The NO escaped before I could catch it, and then I did cry, hot little drops, and I begged.

"You mention one more goddamn word about the Nightmare Man, and you don't see your precious granny again," she said, grabbed my chin and hissed like a snake.

Julie left. She and Ben never came home from school. Some of her clothes were missing and some pictures. I found a note under my pillow that just says Sorry. I can't anymore. The knife is next to it. I put the knife back before I call 911.

The police come and take a report. One of them is a lady with crooked bottom teeth and a bun at the bottom of her neck. She asks me about Julie, about Ben, and I answer.

"Do you know why Julie would want to run away?" she asks. Her eyes invade me, and I want to tell her about the Nightmare

Man and the rest of everything that eats me up inside.

But our secrets swell up and choke me. I shake my head and look down. "She hates everything here," I say instead.

"Here?" She looks around the crappy house.

"Everywhere," I say. "She wants to live by the beach."

She nods.

They find Julie and bring her back. She doesn't cry. She sits silent beside me on the couch while the police talk to mom.

"Did you tell?" she asks.

I shake my head and pull stuffing out of the couch, put it back.

"I'm going to kill myself," she says. "There's no escaping here."

The Nightmare Man isn't so scary in the light.

He opens his eyes, and his wet worm mouth, when I stab him.

The knife sticks out and blood trickles around it. I thought there would be more. His mouth opens and closes, no sounds.

I thought it would work right away. I thought he would wink out and disappear, like in a fairy tale.

His hands fix around the knife and pull it out. Blood gushes, and he dies.

He leaves behind his human face. Maybe I always knew.

I call the number on the back of the card the crooked teeth officer left me.

"It's Daisy Beasley. I need you to come to get me." I hang up.

She comes, and I am sitting on the concrete steps. I have a book beside me, the longest one I could find. I hope they will let me read, wherever I am going.

Her eyes get wide at the blood that's on my clothes.

"Oh, Daisy, are you alright?" she says. She hits the thing on her shoulder. "Unit 17, I need medics now."

"I killed the Nightmare Man," I say. "So he wouldn't hurt Julie anymore. She was going to kill herself if he didn't stop."

"Are you hurt, Daisy? Did he hurt you?"

"No. And sometimes."

"Who is the Nightmare Man, Daisy? Where is he?"

"Inside."

"Are you sure he's dead? I need to check," she says, hand on her weapon, pushing beside me. "Who was he?"

But she's past me now, shouldering inside.

I sit back on the steps and pick up my book.

Julie won't have any more bad dreams.

Ennigaldi

By Sam Schreiber

S AY THERE is a small child trying to get his mother's attention while they wait for the subway. It's late, and she is tired, which is why she doesn't notice when he wanders toward the edge of the platform, a foot or two from where you are standing. You consider saying something, but before you have the chance, the child slips on his shoelaces.

There's a familiar rumble beneath your feet. The headlamp of an approaching train begins to glow around the corner of the tunnel. The child's arms windmill as he tries to regain his balance.

This is where things get tricky. In one version of the story, you drop to your knees, catch the child by the arm, and pull him to safety. His mother turns just in time to see it happen. She rushes to her son, hugs his body to hers, and gushes with gratitude, which you accept before boarding the train. The two of them remain on the platform. Understandable. Only the child's mother saw what you did. She doesn't know your name, and you don't know hers. But for the rest of the night, and in years to come, you play the scene back in your mind. It's a simple, private reassurance, and it gets you through some dark moments.

Then there's the second version of the story. You reach out for the child, but this time his arm rebounds off yours. You will never know whether he would have regained his balance on his own or not. What you do know is that it is your touch that shifts his center of gravity over the train tracks. The child tucks and rolls, landing harmlessly the way children sometimes do. But you already know he only has seconds left.

His mother screams as the train pulls into the station. Did she see you were trying to save her son? Or from her vantage point, did it look as though it was all your fault? You'll never know. You ran. Up the cement steps, out onto the street, for blocks on end. You expected sirens. They never came. But for the rest of the night and in years to come, you play that moment back in your mind. It's where your thoughts invariably arrive during dark moments.

What's the difference between these two stories? Is it that in one you are fast and graceful while in the other you are slow and clumsy? That you had a good night's sleep the night before or stayed out late with friends? That you overexerted yourself at the gym that morning or stopped for a cocktail earlier that evening? Is it a question of luck? Or are these two stories fragments of the same reality, like white light separated by a prism into its constituent colors?

The answer doesn't matter just now. But it will.

There is no dust in the museum. At least none you can feel when you run your fingers over the wood panels and glass displays. You've developed a theory or two on the subject. The museum has no discernible weather, and you are becoming increasingly certain there are no working exits or entrances. If there was no particulate matter in the museum to begin with, and only you to bring any in from the outside, is it any wonder there's none to be found now?

Of course, there are an awful lot of assumptions baked into that explanation. Not to mention unanswered questions. How you arrived in the museum to begin with barely scratches the surface. But science never was your strong suit, and, in any event, the museum's conspicuous cleanliness is the least of its mysteries.

Another thing the museum doesn't have is a map. At least not of itself. You have found maps of other things. Charts dated from the mid-1980s onward detailing your progress from one small town in the Pacific Northwest to another. There was a sepia-colored globe that filled up an entire room with broken red lines painted between Chicago and Glasgow (your cousin's wedding, which you attended in your late twenties), Bend, Oregon and Manhattan (your summer internship between your sophomore and junior year of college) and a few other places. But there is nothing at all relating to the museum's layout. Which isn't to say there isn't a certain curatorial logic to the exhibits and their relative position to one another. There is. But it's a logic you've had to piece together on your own.

The Hall of Wine, for example, where a thousand or so empty green bottles form a series of pyramids, branches off into dozens of different hallways. One predictably leads to a split-level garden filled with empty fifths of whiskey, rum, and other spirits. Another leads to the Hall of Sex, where hundreds of used prophylactics and their wrappers are pinned against corkboards like pressed butterflies. Other more risqué souvenirs sit atop pedestals beneath warm pink and blue lights. Still another passage leads down a flight of stairs to a library of books you have read, books you meant to finish, and books that sat un-racked on your shelf, all maddeningly encased behind thick glass. Like dust and maps, the museum is very much short on readable texts.

One thing the museum does have is gravity. You walk down the halls rather than float through them. There is up, and there is down. From this, you tentatively postulate that the museum has a top floor and a bottom floor, though you have yet to successfully discover either. Then again, you sometimes wonder if the museum might not be some sort of Möbius strip or donut-shaped structure in space, and that should you ascend high enough you would merely arrive at the museum's "lowest" floor, and vice versa. It's pure conjecture, really. As far as you know, the museum could extend infinitely in every direction.

But, of course, that would make no sense. Even if you don't understand the museum's purpose, you've learned enough to grasp its overarching theme. And no life, no matter how well-lived, extends so far.

Forget the child. The child was not the point of the story. He existed simply to disappear as the train pulled away from the platform. Or to die gruesomely beneath its wheels. In either case, the point of the story was you. Or rather, the two yous. The you whose life is elevated by the experience and the you whose life is shattered by it.

But of course, there are more than just two of you, aren't there? In point of fact, there are large and small infinities of you ebbing and flowing across the fulcrum of reality like cosmic tide. There are some who find this concept comforting. It's a metaphysical card trick, a way of forgetting that no matter how you measure the ride, oblivion waits for you at the end of it.

But imagine the barriers between the various iterations of you were to fall. Imagine nations of you finding common cause among one another, forging alliances, breaking them, fighting for dominance as every passing moment makes it clearer and clearer that you are all running out of real estate in which to exist.

Too abstract? Then imagine returning home to find your lover murdered by some other iteration of you, perhaps to nudge you onto a path that suits their needs or perhaps in retaliation for a slight that yet a third iteration of you committed. Imagine finding your house, your office, or the city where you live burned down to its bedrock and knowing some other version of you is responsible. Better still, imagine watching through a collapsing aperture between realities as the fabric of space and time in a neighboring universe tears itself apart and knowing, with grim certainty, that you have done the right thing. Or at least what needed to be done.

Sit with that for a moment. The rest of us will wait.

While it is possible to retrace your steps in the museum, it is not necessary in any strict sense. There are no dead ends. Every exhibit leads to another exhibit, mostly through twisting, circuitous paths. You would kill for a compass, a pad of paper, and something to write with. You lifted the Naugahyde divan from your grandfather's study in Pittsburgh and lobbed it against the glass protecting your journal from the seventh grade. The glass held. The Kennesaw multi-tool you brought with you to summer camp has a compass in it, but again, the glass—if it even is glass—proved unbreakable. Not everything in the museum is shielded or out of reach. Just the things you want.

You can't say for sure where you are in relation to where you started. Where and when you started is something you are less and less sure of. You are thirty, maybe forty floors below the now-pristine 1986 Toyota you totaled off the New Jersey turnpike. Two, maybe three miles east of the black room with the bleached white skeletons of two guinea pigs, three cats, a smattering of goldfish, and a Boston Terrier, all hanging in various poses by hooks and monofilament. Plaster impressions, you thought at first, but the dog's parietal bone was surprisingly coarse to the touch.

That was the last time you recall turning around and going back the way you came. It was when you realized that the deeper into the museum you went, the less you cared for the exhibits. By deeper, you think you mean further in any particular direction. But you could be wrong about that.

Nonetheless, you have decided to try for the museum's bottom-most level. This is not as easy as it sounds. Staircases are rarer than hallways, and they don't always go in the correct direction. Progress is frustratingly slow, but you have been disciplined. It could be your imagination, but the air feels ever so slightly danker the lower you descend. No drops of condensation forms against the glass displays, but there is something softer and hazier about your surroundings. Or maybe it's a trick of the light.

The vault takes you by surprise when you find it. It's a domed space easily a thousand feet high, at the bottom of a spiral staircase that takes many hours to descend. Blocks of buildings stretch out beneath the purplish black stone ceiling. Every house you've ever lived in, every office you've ever worked in, every store you've stepped foot in, even the Statue of Liberty, which you visited when you were ten years old. They're all present and accounted for, though there's no obvious rhyme or reason to their layout. You can't enter any of the buildings, of course. The doors rattle when you try them, but each one is locked. Not exactly a surprise at this stage.

You do not arrive at the vault's edge, but rather, you suspect, at its center. The structure you find there is an obelisk of sorts. A hexagonal cone the same dark shade as the vault itself, which you suppose is how it managed to sneak up on you. It seems as though it should reach all the way up to the top of the vault, but it tapers off to a point instead. Deep grooves make crude parallelograms in the floor beneath your feet and begin to glow white hot as you approach the epicenter of the vault, perhaps of the museum itself.

The obelisk appears to have six faces, at least at first. But the longer you look, the more you sense there is more to the story. Six is the organizing principle perhaps, but just as a cartoon figure represents more than the two-dimensional lines making up its composition, so too does the Obelisk represent more than its protrusion into the three-dimensional space you occupy.

You wait a very long time. Longer, you think, than you spent descending into the vault. You can't be sure, but it feels as though the other faces of the obelisk—not just the other five but *all* the other faces—are coming alive. Then the Obelisk begins to move. Its faces are sluggish as they turn on an invisible axis, tilt on their side, and open with a low, stone groan. Your fingers twitch, as if remembering how to sign your name.

Say there was a Sumerian princess who was also the high priestess of Sin and the headmistress of an entirely different order of priestesses in the city of Ur. Her name was Ennigaldi and, more importantly than any of that, she was the curator of the world's first museum. Or so historians and archeologists tell us. What they often fail to mention, or perhaps even grasp, is the full extent of *why this mattered.*

Understand that without Ennigaldi, there would be no such thing as a university. No such thing as a library. We may have stumbled into some understanding of the sciences and poetry without her assistance. At the end of the day, human ingenuity is a river cutting a path through the hard rock of an unfriendly, unforgiving world. But that river's path is no forgone conclusion. There are moments—and make no mistake, we're discussing one now—when history doesn't simply happen. It is written into being.

For you, it might have been baseball cards, vinyl records, or out-of-print novels. Your mother's jewelry or your children's crayon drawings. But at some point in your life, you have reached out to steal a piece of the world, to shield it from the winds of time. To dare the impossible and take up arms against the literal will of the universe.

This desire, this need, is the gift of Ennigaldi.

Well. One of two.

The uncountable faces of the obelisk fan open, and you find yourself climbing a short flight of stone steps. The light from the lettering beneath your feet grows unbearably bright. Before you realize what is happening, whiteness overtakes you.

It is difficult to know exactly when you regain consciousness. Mostly because you are on your back, looking up at a cloudless white sky. The sand beneath your body is black and so are the waves lapping at the shore a short distance away.

No, not waves. You're lying on the bank of a burbling river. On the other side, nearly at the horizon, is a pure white ziggurat. It would be difficult to make out against the sky were it not for the black corona outlining its shape.

You wade into the black water. It's as cold as a lake frozen over in the winter. You should fear for your extremities, for hypothermia, for drowning. But you've begun to understand the time for such worries is over. You let the current take you downstream, making steady progress toward the far shore. It isn't so very different than fighting your way down to the vault or waiting for the obelisk to open. It simply takes patience.

You allow yourself some rest once you climb out of the river. There is no sun in the sky above you, but somehow your clothes dry out slightly after you twist the black water out of them. You're merely wet and not sopping when you continue toward the ziggurat.

It would have been easy to miss the black, vaguely pyramidal extrusion in the sand. It is only six or seven inches high. But there is literally nothing else but the ziggurat to catch your eye. You sit on your haunches to examine it. Plastic, you realize, with pale scuff marks and…you squint. The letters RCA encircled by an oval are embossed on the side. You excavate around the extrusion with your fingers and then your hands, finding the sand gives way.

When you were three years old, you stood atop your parents' television set. Physical bravery was more your style at that age than any other.

"No more Sesame Street," your mother said sternly as she swept up the broken shards of the screen from the floor. You were too stunned by the tumble you'd taken minutes earlier to object. Unlike your Toyota, the TV still shows signs of the abuse. The screen, you discover as you pull the set out of the sand, is cracked and spiderwebbed. One of the rabbit ear antennae is bent at an odd angle and the power cord hangs limply from the oak-colored box.

"I think what Robbe-Grillet is getting at is the artist's need to sign their work," you hear a voice crackle. You drop the television back into the sand as if it had shocked you. Warped green and purple shapes fluctuate behind the broken glass as the voice continues through damaged speakers.

"It's not showing off. Not exactly. It's more like carving your name in a tree. Telling the world you were there. You can't do that in a way that you're sure is going to make any sense to anyone else ten, twenty, a hundred years from now. The world has to meet you on your terms."

There's nearly as much static as there is signal, but you can't pretend you don't recognize the voice that is speaking.

"Certainly one way of looking at things," you hear a second voice chuckle.

The screen dies with a quiet thump. Blackness converges on its center, leaving a single fading point of light. You shake the set, but it's no use.

The answer is yes, by the way. The version of you who saved the child on the subway platform and the one who may or may not have been responsible for his death. They're both real. They both happened. They're both you. They both enter Ennigaldi's obelisk. They both find themselves at the foot of her ziggurat.

You all do. Eventually.

The corona isn't black, you realize as you approach the ziggurat. It's every color of the spectrum, from piercing violet to warm red. But it's easy to see how you made the mistake. It's as if the ziggurat is perfectly positioned to occlude some distant, impossibly radiant black star.

You consider walking past the ziggurat to see if you're correct. You've come this far, after all. But something inside you clenches uneasily at the thought. Even here, at the end of everything, there are limits. Not every television set is meant to be dug up.

The entrance to the ziggurat is an archway. The light from the sky fades away as you turn the corner inside. The black sand beneath your feet is now black marble. The alabaster walls are impossibly illuminated by light with no source, just like in the museum. You've returned. Perhaps you never left.

"This is what we mean when we talk about the aesthetic of collection," you hear a voice echo from down the hall. "It isn't meant to be natural. It's humanity's imprint *upon* nature."

You follow the sound down the hall and find yourself entering an amphitheater. Upon the proscenium, sitting atop a column about five and a half feet high, sits your old clock radio. Your voice, a little reedier than it sounds in your own ears, continues to recite your graduate thesis.

"And yes. It is reasonable to view this imprint as fundamentally oppositional. The universe is an entropic place. We are, at the end of the day, a parade of ephemerality marching towards nothingness. Which makes the Collector something altogether different than what we have previously conceived of."

You walk toward the podium. Your recorded voice takes on a more stentorian quality as it finds the rhythm of your address.

"We like to think of the Collector as incurably afraid of breaking the rules. Remove Kenner's Obi-Wan Kenobi doll from its original packaging? Blasphemy! Touch an original print of Action Comics Number One without gloves? Death is too kind a fate!"

You approach the clock radio. Like the television set, its power cord dangles freely. You wonder what would happen if you smashed the device against the proscenium floor.

"But consider: the Collector is, first and foremost, a rule-breaker. There is an established order to human existence, and objects are relegated well below people. We may not always act like it, but we understand that a man may buy a priceless Fabergé egg from a private collector simply for the pleasure of crushing it beneath his boot. We understand that if a maniac threatens to kill a human being or set fire to a Samuel Johnson dictionary, we'll do our best to protect the book, but the life of the hostage comes first. What sets the Collector apart from the rest of humanity is their willingness to subordinate the animal below the artifact. It's not simply rebellion – it's perversion!"

You pick up the clock radio from its column. Feel your voice vibrating through the beige plastic encasement. On the face of the podium, beneath where the clock radio sat, there is the relief of a naked woman perched atop two lions, flanked by two owls, with wings and talons like a harpy's. The lines of her face are elegant in their sphinxlike simplicity. Empty white eyes look up at you with surprising warmth.

"And yet what we must not forget is that the Collector is emphatically interested in the fruits of human endeavor. What we create. What we admire. What we worship, in one fashion or another. Our holy relics. It would be a mistake to think of the Collector as indifferent to human drama, to the messiness of the organic. No, what we must understand is that the ethos of the Collector is, at long last, the ethos of immor-"

You let the clock radio slide from your hands. It clatters to the floor, cutting off your last words. You would sob if any part of you was still capable of it. The proscenium, you realize dully, is an enclosure unto itself. There's nowhere left to go but back the way you came.

Trauma Narrating

By Dr. Raymond Thoss

"FOR AGES they had been without lives of their own. The whole of their being was open to the world and nothing divided them from the rest of creation. How long they had thus flourished none of them knew. Then something began to change . . . The epoch had passed when the whole of their being was open to the world and nothing divided them from the rest of creation . . . For ages they had been without lives of their own. Now that they had such lives there was no turning back. The whole of their being was closed to the world, and they had been divided from the rest of creation. Nothing could be done about that, having as they did lives of their own. But something would have to be done if they were to live with that which *should not be* . . ."[1]

. . . Then.

Something else occurred. Something that may have been a product of the tragedy, of that which should not be, of the trauma of the curse of consciousness. As Pandora found a tool, a weapon, against all the horrors unleashed on the world, the First Ones at the dawn of consciousness found such a tool, such a weapon. Like the Trauma that had been unleashed on them, this tool, this weapon, was nothing they could hold in their hands. It was the Narrative. The Story. The Trap. It was a way to trap the trauma, to rebel, as Lucifer had done in Milton's fable, against the injustice done to them. Over oceans of time they would learn how to use this weapon against the trauma, the damnation, which they never asked for, but could never escape. Yet the Conspiracy dictated that as soon as the First Ones were made aware of this trap, this tool, this weapon, they were supposed to be incapacitated, lulled back to sleep, by being told the following:

"You're not supposed to talk about _____."

Fill in the blank.

That phrase is what countless people have said to me as well as the children I work with.

I find that statement deeply ironic because across both adult[2] and child[3] trauma treatment science, there comes a point where, in

---

[1] Thomas Ligotti, *The Conspiracy Against the Human Race* (New York: Hippocampus Press, 2010), 19-20.

[2] Christine A. Courtois and Julian D. Ford, *Treatment of Complex Trauma, A Sequenced, Relational-Based Approach* (New York: Guilford, 2013); as well as Patricia A. Resick, Candice M. Monson, and Kathleen M. Shard, *Cognitive Processing Therapy for PTSD: A Comprehensive Manual* (New York: Guilford, 2017).

[3] Judith A. Cohen, Anthony P. Mannarino, and Esther Deblinger, *Treating Trauma*

order to "resolve" one's traumatic stress, one must "tell their story." Judith Herman, one of the pioneers in the field of trauma therapy, calls this "Mourning and Reconciliation.[4]" If you remember one thing from this discussion, it should be this: being heard is the opposite of being traumatized. Despite the almost unanimous agreement in the field that, at some point, one should "tell their story," empirical literature has a paucity of scientific consensus of the nuts and bolts of *how* to do this. Indeed, the first thing many patients tell me when we start therapy is "I don't want to tell my story again." When I ask why, they usually tell me they have tried to do it before, and it was a horrible experience. One of the biggest "rookie mistakes" I see a beginning trauma therapist commit is to make a client "tell their story" as the first thing they do in treatment. This would be akin to going into surgery with no anesthetic, the physician simply slashing with no plan or preparation or understanding. The line between skilled surgeon and butcher (regarding the component of "telling one's story") is often very, very fine in actual psychological practice in the real world.

This often results in the most counter-therapeutic encounter possible. Instead of being heard, the patient was forced to speak. That is not splitting hairs; it is a life and death distinction. I have seen patients attempt suicide multiple times *after* receiving "trauma therapy" in large part because they were forced to speak vs. being heard. The state of the field calls the process of "telling one's story," Trauma Narrating. It is also important to note that one of the core

---

and *Traumatic Grief in Children and Adolescents, 2nd Edition* (New York: Guilford, 2017); as well as Margaret E. Blaustein and Kristine M. Kinniburgh, *Treating Traumatic Stress in Children and Adolescents* (New York: Guilford, 2010).

[4] Judith Herman, *Trauma and Recovery* (Philadelphia: Basic Books, 1992).

distinctions to make is that even though we will talk of "trauma narratives," the term "Trauma Narrating" is key. Telling one's story is verb, not noun. This seemingly trivial distinction is central to the story being able to be an effective weapon. A Trauma Narrative is the result (noun) of the action (verb) of Trauma Narrating just as the gauze and blood on the operating floor is the result of the surgical procedure. The Narrative is the fist that connects but the Narrating is the rotation of the body that gives the power. "Narrative Therapy" as a term has empirical precedence,[5] but I would argue that its roots are as deep as Gilgamesh. The two types of stories that are typically identified in the trauma therapy literature are Focal Memory Narratives[6] and Thematic Narratives.[7] Respectively, they represent narratives about a focal incident or person and narratives about a theme, core belief, or Schema. I will posit, from my clinical experience, a third form: Symbolic Narratives. These are narratives about something much stronger than a single person's focal incident or a core belief. These are narratives about concepts that transcend time and space.

A central thesis of this article is that the field of trauma therapy (specifically the "Trauma Narrating" component) can benefit from a close analysis of the literature of what is called "The Weird." It is also a central thesis that Thomas Ligotti is one of the few writers in history that effectively narrates across all three narrative structures

---

[5] For example, Michael White and David Epston, *Narrative Means to Therapeutic Ends* (New York: W.W. Norton and Company, 1990).

[6] Edna B. Foa, Elizabeth A. Hembree, and Barbara Olasov Rothbaum, *Prolonged Exposure Therapy for PTSD* (Oxford: Oxford University Press, 2007).

[7] Judith A. Cohen, Anthony P. Mannarino, Matthew Kleithermes, and Laura A. Murray. "Trauma-Focused CBT for Youth with Complex Trauma," *Child Abuse and Neglect* 36 (2012): 528-541.

cited, and, as a corollary, has rich material that can be mined for Trauma Narrating in live fire clinical practice. Although other authors will be discussed across all three structures, this article will show that Thomas Ligotti is the paradigm by which Trauma Narrating as a field of science, and "The Weird" as a field of literature, can be brought to synergistic union for the healing of the abused and neglected patients I work with, the healing of those told "You're not supposed to talk about _____."

Before we proceed, a few notes. First, whether a particular author fits "best" in one of the three taxonomies is not the central, or even peripheral, focus of this discussion. It would be like arguing whether a particular edged weapon fits "best" as a knife or a sword or a spear. What is important is *that* it cuts and *how* it cuts. A goal of this discussion is to see how the literature of the Weird can inform the healing of the shattered in the most under-scrutinized portion of trauma therapy science, the Trauma Narrating component. Function, not academic taxonomy, is what is important in this specific discussion. I am mindfully using Ligotti as the paradigm; reasons why will become evident as we discuss the three domains. That is not to say there are not others. That is also not to say that I have a certain author "right" in my taxonomy.

Second, one of my mentors said that a good article is a starting point, not an ending point. I hope that part of this discussion inspires others to see where an author "fits" and, more importantly to me, how that author's Trauma Narrating tools can be extrapolated to help the traumatized. Third, this same mentor told me that as a psychologist it would benefit me to take the words "right" and "wrong" out of my lexicon as a doctor and put in "closer" and "farther." Whether I got a certain writer, or Ligotti, himself, "right" is not as important to me as whether I get "closer" to finding a synergistic union between the literature of "The Weird" and the science of "Trauma Narrating" that ultimately helps a tortured child I am working with. Stories are as old as humankind. In essence, with both this first and second response, I am issuing the central challenge of this article. The challenge for discussions that move closer to this synergism, closer to the tool, the weapon, that can shatter the Conspiracy.

Let us begin.

Section 1: Focal Memory Narratives – The Leaf

It may be helpful to present the tripartite structure. The tripartite structure is as follows:

1. Focal Memory Narratives[8]
2. Thematic Narratives[9]

---

[8] A representative example can be found in Edna B. Foa, Elizabeth A. Hembree, and Barbara Olasov Rothbaum, *Prolonged Exposure Therapy for PTSD* (Oxford: Oxford University Press, 2007).

[9] Representative examples for children and adults, respectively, can be found in Judith A. Cohen, Anthony P. Mannarino, Matthew Kleithermes, and Laura A. Murray. "Trauma-Focused CBT for Youth with Complex Trauma" *Child Abuse and Neglect* 36 (2012): 528-541; and Christine A. Courtois and Julian D. Ford, *Treatment of Complex Trauma, A Sequenced, Relational-Based Approach* (New York: Guilford, 2013).

3. Symbolic Narratives (look like #1 but does not respond, and may be exacerbated by, the tools used for #1 and #2)

    a. There is no citation in either the psychological or the trauma literature for this. It is not spoken of in the empirical literature but is spoken of in literature and philosophy.[10]

The focus of this specific section is the first: focal memory narratives. These are narratives in which the story focuses on a single incident (e.g., the last incident of sexual assault in a patient) or person (e.g., my father's death). In the work of Thomas Ligotti, this is best represented by the story "The Frolic," a *specific* narrative of an evening in a family's home. Ligotti has said that although this story is often cited by people as the first Ligotti story they read (primarily due to being the first story in both *Songs of a Dead Dreamer* as well as *The Nightmare Factory*) he is not necessarily a fan of it, describing its birth as "Desperate to get one of my stories published, I finally broke down and wrote about some normal characters living a normal life. The result was 'The Frolic.'"[11] Ligotti highlighted that he took the perspective of the "normal" family vs. the "abnormal" John Doe. He stated that he felt he had to do this, or it simply would never get published. One interpretation is that a standard focal narrative is "what the people want." This is not to say

---

[10] Ernst Cassirer, in his magnum opus, *The Philosophy of Symbolic Forms* talks at length about this. Cassirer is quick to admit that he is not the first, and will not be the last (e.g., his successor, Susanne K. Langer produced incredible contributions) to discuss how the Symbol is used in human interactions.

[11] Thomas Ligotti, Introduction, *The Frolic: Short Film Screenplay*, Frolic, LLC, 2007, vi-vii.

that "The Frolic" is a bad story. In fact, it is quite good. But Ligotti's (correct) point is that it is LIMITED—limited by the confines of this focal "normal" narrative. Specifically, he stated, "One thing I learned from writing 'The Frolic:' most readers find horror stories scarier when normal characters are placed front and center than when they are shoved into the background or absent entirely. For these readers, naturally enough, scariness is more coveted than any other element of a horror story, including imagination, ideas, prose style, and atmosphere."[12]

An alternate example would benefit us. I offer Laird Barron as the most consistent, perhaps strongest, proponent of the focal memory narrative. *The Light is the Darkness* is a wonderful example. Barron, mindfully, incorporates the noir elements into his narratives with devastatingly effective results, as Mike Mignola, creator of *Hellboy*, incorporates old pulp tropes with equally devastating effectiveness. Implicit in the noir and pulp tradition that both Barron and Mignola reshape so well is the standard emphasis on conventional focal narration. There are characters. There is plot. There is a who, a what, a when, a where; and there is an easily identified beginning, middle, and end, even if the ending is often cosmic (as in *The Light is the Darkness*).

It is here that we come to the first lesson that we can cull from the intersection between the Weird and Trauma Therapy. In trauma therapy we often hear a variation on the Lovecraftian "unnameable." Part of the trauma therapist's job is to create a specific (who, what, when, where) and coherent (beginning, middle, end) narrative of the traumatic event because our children and adults say that what happened to them is so bad they literally cannot talk about it, cannot

---

[12] Ibid., vii-viii.

give it words. The structure of a focal memory narrative is put in place to accomplish the goal of "trapping" the trauma, taking away the "heat" from the memory. One of my colleagues likens the process of how the focal memory narrative captures the pain within the story to an insect being caught in amber. This is an ancient idea. Some Native American tribes believe they can capture the pain, not only of an individual person but of the entire tribe, in a story.

Herein lie the two sides of the coin of the focal memory narrative. Specifically, the problems with focal narratives in literature (as Ligotti cited regarding "The Frolic") are the exact virtues of focal narratives in trauma therapy. Its strength is its weakness (in literature) and its weakness is its strength (in trauma therapy). I call it the rollercoaster. The first time one rides the roller coaster it is frightening. The second time, perhaps still frightening, but not so much. The third, fourth, fifth, etc., the effect significantly wears off. One either finds another roller coaster or simply is done with the roller coaster. In trauma therapy this is called desensitization. It is the same psychological technique used for phobias and OCD, but the primary difference is that instead of being used on something tangible (e.g., spiders or hand washing) it is used on something intangible (i.e., the specific focal *memory*). Its technical term is "exposure therapy"[13] and its job is to make the intangible (memory) tangible (a story written down in front of you). C. Hall Thompson in his weird tale, "Spawn of the Green Abyss" perfectly captures how desensitization works when his protagonist says, "For, now, I had at least one thing for which to be grateful.

---

[13] Edna B. Foa, and Barbara O. Rothbaum, *Treating the Trauma of Rape* (New York: Guilford, 1998).

The evil that I fought had taken on concrete form; I was no longer fighting shadows."[14] This. This is where the focal memory narrative draws its power; it makes the shadows concrete.

This is simultaneously one of the chief complaints, as well as one of the chief virtues, for people who hate or love, respectively, these types of narratives in the field of the Weird. Specifically, that there IS a concrete form. John Doe is the "villain" in "The Frolic." Conrad Navarro in "The Light is the Darkness" starts with concrete antagonists as is typical of pulp and noir literature (in his case the fighters in the "Pageant") and finishes with something concrete in the dénouement (even though it has cosmic overtones). This is at maximum effectiveness the first time. The effect wears off quickly after this. This is a fault in weird fiction, a virtue in trauma therapy. Ligotti points this out incisively when he says, "scariness is more coveted than any other element of a horror story, including imagination, ideas, prose style, and atmosphere."

The first time a patient tells me their focal memory narrative they are typically in high distress. One of my supervisors, using a technique called "Prolonged Exposure," had a trashcan by the chair patients would sit in. I asked her why it was there. She said, "Wait." The patient came in, started talking about their worst incident of sexual assault and threw up midway through. My supervisor simply said, "Continue." The patient did. To my great surprise they reported feeling significantly better at the end of session. This is the power of desensitization; which is a core lesson of the Focal Memory Narrative.

---

[14] C. Hall Thompson "Spawn of the Green Abyss" in *A Mountain Walked: Great Tales of the Cthulhu Mythos* ed. by S. T. Joshi (Lakewood: Centipede Press, 2014), 83.

But.

Working in the field, one finds its limitations. The Masters of the Weird, like Thomas Ligotti, are well aware of its limitations. Trauma therapy is only beginning to find its limitations. The field still has arguments that desensitization may be the primary tool to heal the traumatized.[15] But. The focal memory narrative is a leaf. When one encounters the tree, one sees the limitations more clearly.

Section 2: Thematic Narratives – The Tree

The focus of this section is number two, thematic narratives. These are narratives in which the story focuses not on a single incident or person (not a simple who, what, when, where) but on an underlying theme. In Cognitive-Behavioral Therapy (CBT) a theme is used interchangeably with the technical terms "Core Beliefs" or "Schema."[16] A Theme/Core Belief/Schema is a unifying belief that says something fundamental about the individual, the individual's world (anything from Earth to "my family"), and/or the individual's future.[17] Schemas are amoral. They can be positive or negative. They are also *deep* within your neurology. I will demonstrate with a

---

[15] Carmen P. McLean and Edna B. Foa. "Prolonged Exposure Therapy for Posttraumatic Stress Disorder: A Review of Evidence and Dissemination" *Expert Reviews of Neurotherapeutics* 11 (2011): 1151-1163.

[16] Jeffrey E. Young, Janet S. Klosko, and Marjorie E. Weishaar, *Schema Therapy: A Practitioner's Guide* (New York: Guilford, 2003).

[17] Ibid.

positive Schema: "I love my child." Those of you reading this who have children could give me an analytic proof for why you love your child, but that is kind of me missing the whole point. Because that "belief" is not 100% frontal lobe. No, it goes deeper into your neurology. Jeff Young talks about how Achemas access frontal lobe, but also midbrain.[18] For instance, you can remember the weight of your child when he/she was born, as well as the smell of his/her hair when you bathed them as an infant. Schemas/themes/core beliefs are wired into deep recesses of your brain.

I first encountered the negative type with the first child I ever worked with who had trauma. He was a sixteen-year-old Hispanic male who had multiple, as well as chronic, traumatic events. There was nothing focal about this kid. Those reading this who are parents probably tell their children some variation of "I love you. You're great! You're gonna have a good day." This child, however, told me that for the first eight years of his life his father would find him at least once a day (even if he was asleep) and tell him the following: "You're stupid. You're ugly. I wish you were never born." Let us go through his Schemas.

Self: His exact statement was "I was slow. I was weak. I was stupid." When I first encountered him at sixteen he was training to become a weapon. Boxing, martial arts, weight lifting, wrestling, jiu-jitsu, kickboxing.

World: I remember when he told me the following: "Man, don't you know that there are only two types of people in the world? Those who get hurt and those who do the hurting." When I tried (abysmally) to challenge this, he looked at me like I was naïve and sheltered.

---

[18] Ibid.

Future: He had a pretty good argument. Some of the local gangs were literally gunning for him. He believed he would be dead by the time he was eighteen years old.

With all the distorted Schemas one would expect him to be near catatonic. Nope. In DSM-V PTSD criteria standard PTSD has terms such as "Hyperarousal" or "Re-experiencing." Focal Memory Narratives are hard-wired, and quite effective, at dealing with hyperarousal or re-experiencing symptoms, with classical DSM-V PTSD. If we take a stress scale from 1 to 10, with 1 being minimal stress and 10 being maximum stress, classic DSM-V PTSD patients typically come in with a 10 out of 10, similar to my supervisor's patient who threw up in the treatment session. This is an individual who is high on hyperarousal and/or re-experiencing symptoms.[19] That was NOT my sixteen-year-old. He was typically at a 1 out of 10. He would even talk about his trauma this way: "So my grandpa, the only good guy I knew, died when I was four. I saw him die. No big. I was raped by a neighbor from like six years old to eight years old at least twice a week. What's that? Couple hundred rapes? Whatevs. Then my dad tried to kill me the first time when I was eight, second time when I was ten, third time when I was..." He may as well have been talking about the weather. Unlike C. Hall Thompson's focal narrative example, my kid was still fighting shadows when I met him. There was nothing concrete to lock on to. It was not that he was without concrete examples. Quite the contrary; he had many. Too many. So many that they *defied*

---

[19] Note that there are two other criteria in DSM-V PTSD criteria: avoidance (C cluster) and negative moods and cognitions (D cluster). I am highlighting B cluster (re-experiencing) and E cluster (hyperarousal) in this discussion (vs. giving an extensive definition of DSM-V PTSD criteria).

concretization. Therefore, it became something not concrete. Something intangible. Something deeper.

It wasn't until I was well into my training, almost a decade after I saw my sixteen-year-old, that I found out what the technical term was for what I saw and why Focal Memory Narratives bounced off kids and adults like him like bullets off Superman. The patient my supervisor had who threw up had standard DSM-V PTSD. My sixteen-year-old had what is called "Complex PTSD," also known as "Complex Trauma."[20] These are technical terms. The one sentence summary for how Complex Trauma differs from standard DSM-V PTSD is that for those with Complex Trauma, their traumas often occurred in the context of relationships; therefore, their healing will occur in the context of relationships; therefore, their "triggers" are often relational in nature. So, these children and adults do not jump at a loud noise. But they do start swinging if you try to hug them or even compliment them. Humans are dangerous. Humans, in and of themselves, are the trigger. My sixteen-year-old once told me "I like dogs better than humans. Dogs can do some horrible things. But they never do it without a good reason. And they never, ever like doing it." That is the voice of Complex Trauma.[21]

So why do focal memory narratives bounce off them? The one

---

[20] For a much more extensive definition of complex trauma see the National Child Traumatic Stress Network's (NCTSN) Complex Trauma page on their website here: http://nctsn.org/trauma-types/complex-trauma.

[21] The Youth Task Force for the National Center for Traumatic Stress (NCTSN) has produced a video that phenomenologically demonstrates (in the middle of the video) what it is like to have Complex Trauma as an adolescent. In this video three dark figures hover above the girl. The Darkness hovers over the girl. The video can be found on YouTube by typing in "NCTSN Complex Trauma" or the title of the video, "Never Give Up."

sentence answer is that my sixteen-year-old did not need to be desensitized (he already was); he needed to be *sensitized*. On that 1 to 10 stress scale he was at a solid 1. He, to be Shakespearean about it, needed to learn to suffer the slings and arrows of outrageous fortune, not to be numb to them, not to avoid them.

Of the three narrative formats discussed in this article, Thomas Ligotti, quantity-wise, spends most of his time here. He has been slighted for this, for lack of "character development."[22] Whereas character development and plot are essential for focal memory narratives; they are incidental, even accidental, for thematic narratives. What is essential is what the narrative says about self, world, and/or future. Ligotti excels here, and has immensely profound comments on Schemas regarding self, world, and future. He gives us peerless description of a world shattered and broken and WRONG. Unlike focal memory narratives, thematic narratives work not on desensitization but on *sensitization* through a phenomenon called cognitive processing. This is why the "rollercoaster" does not occur in Thomas Ligotti's work. If anything, his effects, like a fine wine, only grow STRONGER with each reading. They do not desensitize like a standard shock horror story. They *sensitize*. They can do this because thematic narratives challenge one's distorted thinking. "I was slow. I was stupid. I was weak." Distorted thinking on par with "everything happens for a reason" or "everything will turn out 'alright' in the end." Ligotti cleans the doors of perception. That is an essential function for a thematic narrative. At the same time, there is a danger for the writer (and this explains perhaps why Ligotti remains "underground,"

---

[22] Aware of this, he sent "The Frolic" to publication with John Doe as the "villain" and the family's perspective as the dominant one.

remains not mainstream, even after his work has gained more recognition). In trauma therapy we talk about burn treatment. I ask trainees what the worst type of burn is. Answer: third-degree burn. I then ask what burns hurt. Answer: first and second-degree. That is because third degree burns cauterize the nerve endings. My sixteen-year-old had the equivalent of psychological third-degree burns. Therefore, he required sensitization, not desensitization. Thomas Ligotti "sensitizes" one to the nightmare of the organism, makes one aware of uncomfortable truths. Such an individual is rarely welcomed.

My idiosyncratic exhibit A for Thomas Ligotti's skill with the Thematic Narrative is "Severini." The plot appears simple and focal with the mysterious, mythic Severini taking center stage. Several other Ligotti stories begin similarly, a type of quest, seeking, for a mysterious figure (e.g., "The Last Feast of the Harlequin," "The Night School," "Teatro Grottesco," etc.). One is cued to something more by a typical Ligottian tactic, the unnamed protagonist. Even if Ligotti gives a protagonist a name in his works, the name is a placeholder, not an essentiality. The "character development" is either an afterthought or no thought at all; mood and atmosphere are paramount, Schema is paramount. Quite rapidly a simple visit takes on metaphysical overtones. In "Severini," one is introduced to the Ligottian theme of "the nightmare of the organism,"[23] as well as other powerful themes such as near the end of the story: "He showed them the way into the nightmare, but he could not show them the way out. There is no way out of the nightmare once you have gone so far into its depths."[24]

---

[23] Thomas Ligotti, *The Nightmare Factory* (New York: Carrol and Graf, 1996), 489.
[24] Ibid, 497.

Note that in "Severini," there are characters. There is plot. A thematic narrative does NOT exclude these. It simply shines its light on something more essential: specifically, a core belief, a theme, a Schema (e.g., "the nightmare of the organism"). This is the primary reason they do not "rollercoaster" upon repeated readings. In fact, they may actually grow in effect upon repeated readings. In empirical psychological literature, the reason is because the cognitive processing tool can either desensitize or sensitize. For Complex Trauma, we mindfully use the sensitization aspect of this tool. Ligotti does as well. Humans are fine with desensitization (the rollercoaster of standard horror novels); but the sensitization to the world as a nightmare, FEELING the nightmare of the organism... No, no this cannot stand in a sane world. Ligotti is a master of this tool, of this weapon. I use his tactics daily.

Lovecraft may be his only peer in this arena. Lovecraft's work is also an excellent example of plot and character not being mutually exclusive—but not the essential components—like a suit on a man. Case in point: the narrators of the "Shadow Out of Time," "The Call of Cthulhu," "At the Mountains of Madness," or "The Shadow Over Innsmouth," could all be interchanged easily with minimal restructuring (vs. Conrad Navarro being interchanged with the protagonist of "The Imago Sequence"). In all his works, it is Lovecraft's statements on self, world, and/or future that are of primary importance. Like Ligotti, he is oft criticized for his "lack" of character development. Yet, for Lovecraft, this is no accident; this is intentional. For it is the themes, the Schemas, that are all important in Lovecraft's corpus.

Self: The theme of "bad blood."

World: The world as cosmically indifferent to humans. We are

NOT special little snowflakes.

Future: The Great Old Ones WILL return. They were here before man, and they will be here after man, like a principle of physics, like entropy incarnate.

Whereas focal narratives are leaves, thematic narratives are trees. They respond to cognitive processing, to counter Schemas on self, world, and/or future. The literature is extensive on the effectiveness of cognitive processing.[25] I would argue that Thomas Ligotti does what the psychologist often fails to do: he meets the broken and shattered in THEIR world.[26] I would estimate, in my clinical experience, if one combined both focal memory narratives and thematic narratives, one would have 95% of the patients I have worked with. Leaves plus Trees. These represent the supermajority of my patients.

But.

There is another level, an even deeper level. This level, ironically, has the least empirical and scientific scrutiny while having the most examination in literature. In my professional experience, it is not common. This is true. So perhaps the third narrative is unimportant. Here is my rebuttal. Approximately 6.6 million children are abused in the US each year.[27] Approximately 8 million adults have PTSD in the US.[28] 5%. That means approximately

---

[25] Stephen Lenz, Brian Bruijn, Nina Serman, and Laura Bailey. "Effectiveness of Cognitive Processing Therapy for Treating Posttraumatic Stress Disorder" *Journal of Mental Health Counseling* 36(4) (2014): 360-376.

[26] This is a core thesis in my previous article, "Notes on a Horror."

[27] "Child Abuse Statistics and Facts," Childhelp, Accessed October 8, 2018, https://www.childhelp.org/child-abuse-statistics/

[28] "How Common is PTSD?" U.S. Department of Veterans Affairs, Accessed October 8, 2018, https://www.ptsd.va.gov/public/PTSD-overview/basics/how-common-is-ptsd.asp

330,000 children and 400,000 adults potentially fall into the third narrative structure. Perhaps three quarter of a million individuals merit at least a few pages.

Section 3: Symbolic Narratives – The Forest

Perhaps it is best to start where I first saw a Symbolic Narrative. The first child I worked with who had trauma, the sixteen-year-old I referenced previously. I will repeat what he told me. He said the worst thing that ever happened to him was when he was eight. Late. Driving home from dinner. Pickup truck, single cab, whole family in a line, like ducks on a shooting gallery. Dad driving, mom in the middle, he was near the passenger door. Dad was on some REALLY good stuff. He wanted to kill the mother. As he said, "He was really aiming for her. I was just in the way." Dad opens the door while they are going 60 on the highway headed home. He tries to push mom out the truck. The boy clings on to his mother, so he doesn't fall out of a speeding vehicle on the highway at 60mph. He said, "I saw a 'black river', then we were home." He "lost" time. He said, "I tumbled out of the truck." He turns. Dad pins mom to the bed of the truck, hands around her neck. He's eight. Dad is 250lbs and on drugs. The boy fights. The boy can't win. He runs into the house. He tells his sixteen-year-old brother, "Dad is killing mom!" Brother and brother's friends run out. By that time, dad is gone. Mom is gagging and semi-conscious. Here is where he tells me the thing I can't forget. Ever.

"Everyone was looking at my mom. My brother and his friends. I looked for a second. She was ok. She was breathing. But when I knew she was okay, I looked behind the truck, toward the park near our house. And I saw it. It was my dad, running into the darkness. He looked like a shadow, like a monster. And that's been my whole life. Everyone else looks away from the darkness. Me though, that's my whole life, looking right into the darkness. The Darkness, I'll always be looking into the Darkness." I've never forgotten that.

I've never forgotten that because I spent the rest of my life trying to discover why focal memory narratives and thematic narratives never worked on the type of traumatic stress his memory represented. Both bounced off him.

It took me my entire career to find out why.

I was not dealing with a theme. That description above is a VERY focal memory of a VERY focal incident. Yet, a focal memory narrative (the leaf) for this memory gave him no peace. In fact, talking about this specific memory, his worst one, in the detail that the patient my supervisor had who threw up did not make the boy who saw the Darkness "better." It gave no relief. In fact, it exacerbated the pain. "Talking it out" only made it worse. Cognitive processing and sensitization simply did not work on this specific, worst memory. The state of the art of the trauma treatment literature, all the science we had, told his mental health team it should have made him better. But he was getting worse.

I had no idea what I was dealing with.

Until much later in my career.

I had encountered a Symbol. Symbols do not respond to desensitization as focal memories do (although Symbols often *look like* focal memories). Nor do Symbols respond to cognitive processing/sensitization as Thematic Narratives do. Symbols ONLY respond to "meaning making." Trauma-Focused CBT speaks of meaning making.[29] Literary Hermeneutics is an entire branch of meaning making. Hans Georg Gadamer,[30] to clumsily paraphrase his nuanced work, treats people as texts, and therefore open to interpretation, to meaning making. This concept is not foreign.

The person who hears "meaning making" and thinks "philosophy" may also think "complicated," and, of course, it can go that direction. Yet, it can also be philosophical and simultaneously very simple. Alasdair MacInytre posits that the "plain person" is a philosopher.[31] We need not go even that deep. As I tell my trainees when I am covering this third tool, if you have ever gone through a high school lit course, you can do meaning making. I'll show you. "What's the meaning of *Moby Dick*?" Reply: "It's about a whale. It's about a stupid f-in whale." Ok . . . That's *one* meaning. I would argue a deeply impoverished meaning, but, yes, *a* meaning. Let's try that again. "What's the meaning of *Moby Dick*?" Reply: "I think it's about obsession and, like, even if you get what you're obsessed over, in the end it's totally self-destructive, like you really don't get it and plus you hurt everyone around you." Better. But is that THE meaning of *Moby Dick*? No. The meaning of one of the greatest American novels is inexhaustible. The meaning of one of the worst things a human can do to another is equally

---

[29] Judith A. Cohen, Anthony P. Mannarino, and Esther Deblinger, *Treating Trauma and Traumatic Grief in Children and Adolescents, 2nd Edition* (New York: Guilford, 2017).

[30] Hans Georg Gadamer, *Truth and Method* (New York: Bloomsbury, 2004).

[31] Alasdair MacInytre. "Plain Persons and Moral Philosophy: Rules, Virtues, and Goods," *American Catholic Philosophical Quarterly* 46(1) (1992): 3-19.

inexhaustible. Freud started with the Ancient Greek symbols. His exact choices may have left something to be desired, but the idea of symbols was correct. Even his student, Carl Jung, saw this. The *empirical* literature is silent on symbols, but the literature of psychology actually began with symbols and historically moved away from them.[32] So, we need to look in another well. There is no richer well than the works of Thomas Ligotti regarding the examination and manipulation of symbols.

In *The Agonizing Resurrection of Victor Frankenstein*, Ligotti gives a symphony of Symbolic Narratives. It is critical to note that in *The Agonizing Resurrection*, the pieces look like focal narratives, but are so much more. For instance, "The Blasphemous Enlightenment of Prof. Francis Wayland Thurston, of Boston, Providence, and the Human Race," follows the protagonist of "The Call of Cthulhu" after the incidents of Lovecraft's story. It presents as a focal memory narrative with specificity and coherency, a standard horror story, similar to my sixteen-year-old's. However, Thurston becomes, very rapidly, the symbol for the shattered soul in a world that is literal nightmare. The story ends with "And now nothing can hurt him as he has been so cruelly hurt in the past. Nothing will ever again cause him that pain he suffered so long, an intolerable anguish from which he could never have found release in any other way."[33]

Perhaps his only peer in the Symbolic Narrative is Poe. Poe was a man who, haunted himself, gave beautiful expression to the

---

[32] Brent D. Slife, Bradford J. Wiggins, and Jason T. Graham, "Avoiding and EST Monopoly: Towards a Pluralism of Philosophies and Methods" *Journal of Contemporary Psychotherapy* 35(1) (2005): 83-98.

[33] Thomas Ligotti, *The Agonizing Resurrection of Victor Frankenstein and Other Gothic Tales*, (Eugene: Silver Salamander Press, 1994), 84.

haunted in the human condition. Poe was a master of the Symbolic Narrative. His "Fall of the House of Usher" most clearly illustrates his mastery. Roderick Usher's home exudes decadence down to the stones just as the Usher name, itself, exudes decadence down the generations. Yet an appropriate C. Auguste Dupin can infer an even greater insight by Poe. Specifically, this is Poe's statement on the human condition. We, ourselves, are bile and decay and deceit. No matter how illustrious we once were, we all ultimately decay into the marsh, crumble into the bog. The only blessing we may be granted is a mighty and grand final gasp of decay amid sound and fury, though signifying nothing to the world, signifies everything human. This is Poe's symbolic brilliance with Usher. WE are the symbol. WE are all decay. We are all crumbling, and the only hope in a universe filled with bile is that our house crash to the earth gloriously.

So how did my sixteen-year-old navigate the symbol as he could not desensitize nor sensitize to it? His meaning making went as such: The Darkness was like oil, a very apt comparison given that he lived in West Texas, which is dominated by the oil industry. He stated that when oil was first found it was worthless until someone figured out a way to make an engine. Oil is worthless without the apparatus to harness its power. So, he thought he could use the Darkness for good, could focus it, but would need to build the appropriate apparatus, the appropriate combustion engine. His thought was that oil powers nations, but a long time ago it was just worthless darkness. So, he set about building his metaphysical combustion engine. If this sounds familiar, it should be. Reza Negaresani used the same symbolic imagery for his symbolic narrative in his groundbreaking weird work.[34]

With this new meaning, he harvested the fruit of meaning making: a lesson. He, like me, wanted to hurt the Darkness. and he believed his combustion engine would one day give him the power to do so. Though intangible, he still believed he could hurt the Darkness. His logic was as follows: anything that hurts you must make contact, in some way, shape, or form. Anything that makes contact must have something to contact with in some way, shape, or form. Anything that has something to contact with must be able to contacted in return in some way, shape, or form. And anything you can make contact with, in some way, shape, or form, you, yourself, can hurt. A metaphysical blade through a metaphysical form. He had found the narrative. He had found the tool, the weapon, the trap. He had seen the forest in its entirety.

Section 4: "'In the end?' Nothing ends, Adrian. Nothing ever ends."[35]

I have spent my entire life, decades, honing this tool, this trap, this weapon. It is the only weapon I have ever found that has had any impact whatsoever in this insane nightmare of the world. I, perhaps naively, have presented a nice, clean, packaged structure. In closing,

---

[34] Reza Negarestani, *Cyclonopedia Complicitly with Anonymous Materials* (Melbourne: re.press, 2008).

[35] Alan Moore and David Gibbons, *Watchmen*, Issue 12 (New York: DC Comics, 1987), 27.

I will give only a few clarifications. First, this is NOT a Kantian architectonic. No. This is a passenger on a sinking ship attempting to make a raft from the detritus surrounding him. Which brings me to the second clarification. I hope, that in my hubris, I did not present this as a definitive tripartite structure. No. It is far, far from definitive. The raft may not even float. I present this to you, the listener in the dark, as a call for help, a mayday in the nightmare of existence. Yesterday, I spent two hours talking to counselors who are working the latest school shooting in the United States. The fact that this in no way identifies them or me is one of the tragedies in addition to the obvious. The two-hour conversation was dominated by a simple question: "What do I tell them?" What story do I craft to make the world sane again, to make the world livable again? These counselors asked me for a narrative they could present to the children and families and teachers. As one of my mentors said, "Extreme experiences *demand* a narrative." So, this discussion has not been a definitive presentation on what an "expert" knows; no, it is a call for help from those who have listened from their place in the nightmare. In short, this is not an endpoint but, I hope, a beginning point.

Which brings me to the third clarification. The understanding *that* the weapon works is clear at this point in the science. The understanding *how* the weapon works, and by extension how to improve it, is far from clear. This is my hope from this discussion. The two worlds of those of us who counsel the traumatized and those of us who craft narratives have been siloed for too long. My thought is that it is a part of the Conspiracy that Thomas Ligotti articulates so eloquently. Regardless of its origin, its existence is fact. The knights and the swordsmiths are separated. Both have a critical piece of the only weapon I have ever found to make the Darkness bleed. I spent my whole life looking for weapons against it. Fists don't hurt it. Bullets don't kill it. Only the Narrating, only the narrating has ever hurt the Darkness. It hurt me and mine (perhaps you and yours as well) until there was nothing left of my world. Nothing left but a small, seemingly worthless thing at the bottom of Pandora's box. It was not hope, or maybe it was mistaken for hope. No, it was the Narrating. I end this conversation, this specific narrative, with no definitive answers (my apologies) but with, perhaps, a compass, a direction. The ship is still sinking. I will continue to build my raft. I invite you, and your expertise, to join. The knights and the swordsmiths to come together against the common enemy, against the injustice that was committed at the dawn of humankind, against the Conspiracy. With these last words in my narrative, I will return to listening in the dark, knowing that this is not an end, but a beginning.

Bibliography

Cohen, Judith., Mannarino, Anthony P., and Deblinger, Esther. *Prolonged Exposure Therapy for PTSD.* Oxford: Oxford University Press, 2007.

Cohen, Judith., Mannarino, Anthony P., Kleithermes, Matthew and Murray, Laura A. "Trauma-Focused CBT for Youth with Complex Trauma." *Child Abuse and Neglect* 36, 2012.

Foa, Edna B. and Rothbaum, Barbara O. *Treating the Trauma of Rape.* New York: Guilford, 1998.

Gadamer, Hans George. *Truth and Method.* New York: Bloomsbury, 2004.

Lenz, Stephen., Brujin, Brian., Serman, Nina., and Bailey, Laura. "Effectiveness of Cognitive Processing Therapy for Treating Posttraumatic Stress Disorder." *Journal of Mental Health Counseling* 36(4), 2014.

Ligotti, Thomas. *The Agonizing Resurrection of Victor Frankenstein and Other Tales.* Eugene: Silver Salamander Press, 1994.

— *The Conspiracy Against the Human Race.* New York: Hippocampus Press, 2010.

— Introduction. *The Frolic: Short Film Screenplay*, Frolic, LLC, 2007.

— *The Nightmare Factory.* New York: Carrol and Graf, 1996.

MacIntyre, Alasdair. "Plain Persons and Moral Philosophy: Rules, Virtues, and Goods." *American Catholic Philosophical Quarterly* 46(1), 1992.

McLean, Carmen P. and Foa, Edna B. "Prolonged Exposure Therapy for Posttraumatic Stress Disorder: A Review of Evidence and Dissemination." *Expert Reviews of Neurotherapeutics* 11, 2011.

Moore, Alan and Gibbons, David. *Watchmen*, issue 12. New York: DC Comics, 1987.

Negarestani, Reza. *Cyclonopedia Complicitly with Anonymous Materials.* Melbourne: re.press, 2008.

Slife, Brent D., Wiggins, Bradford J., and Graham, Jason T. "Avoiding and EST Monopoly: Towards a Pluralism of Philosophies and Methods." *Journal of Contemporary Psychotherapy* 35, 2005.

Thompson, C. Hall. "Spawn of the Green Abyss." *A Mountain Walked: Great Tales of the Cthulhu Mythos.* Ed. by S.T. Joshi. Lakewood: Centipede Press, 2014.

Young, Jeffrey E., Klosko, Janet S., and Weishaar, Marjorie E. *Schema Therapy: A Practitioner's Guide.* New York: Guilford, 2003.

credit: Michael Hutter

216

For She is Falling

By John Linwood Grant

S HE IS running.

It is hard to find the green places, but they are there. Sad and railed, smog-ridden, in the centers of city squares. Fern-fronded and tanged with urine in small spaces behind the shops. Glimpses of a broken forest – a single ash tree, with graffiti sprayed on its trunk; an oak which sheds cupped children, only for them to die on paving stones insensible to life.

She dances through them, by them, drawing what she can from a single bold thistle or a tangled rose hedge. These are all she has. Thorn and spike, she borrows them, to be ready.

A busy road, avoided. A grid of houses, sterile traps which shine with a cold light of their own. She turns a corner, confused, only for a man to catch at her, trying to grab her shoulder for some unknown reason. The man's grasping hands shake with ferment, with their false brews.

She does not want to be touched like this and makes it clear with her nails. He winces and draws back; she wild-smiles and shows him the blood on her fingers.

Jump-Nancy keep me, if you watch,
And if you're gone, then come once more.

He holds his torn cheek and makes no move to come near her again. She leaps over a bent metal barrier and into the car-park wastes.

This is a poor land for her. Buckled concrete and oil stains, covered with a rainbow sheen. Hardly a dandelion between slabs of tarmac. Sliding into the lee of a truck, she sniffs the air. It holds the lifeblood of the city – semen and diesel. Both come from the other side of this particular wasteland, two people straining the springs of a rusting vehicle. A less-than man, a sort-of woman.

Somehow, she knows certain things of this place. The words come and go.

Semen and diesel; cash and disgust.

And so, she is running.

"I don't understand," the white-coat says.

But he is unknowing, a world away from hers. There is nothing to understand. They are the mystery; she is passing through. Or she had meant to...

The gleam of a metal box thundering forward as gases explode within it, ice-white eyes that blinded as she hesitated on the great road into the city. No care what was in its path, and so she became chestnut-hard and oak; the glancing impact was less than the breath of moths to her. That's what she kept telling the driver when he finally staggered out, but he smelled of alcohol and sweat. She didn't like being close to him.

"What were you doin' there, stupid bitch!"

By the beaming eyes of his vehicle, then those of a police car, she stood upright.

"You walked, you bloody walked out, right into—"

A police officer gestured him back to his own vehicle, then bent over her.

"We're taking you to hospital, to get you checked out. Alright, miss? What's your name?"

Random faces, unwanted. Words without value.

"Huldre," she said, to the far-off lime trees which were all she had sought.

Take care. Jump-Nancy had the Book of Trees and understood. *This is a proper name to use, but not a safe one.*

"Right, uh, Huldre. Come with us. You might be hurt, uh... inside." For a moment his voice held a father's care.

There were slight cracks in her, it was true, though nothing that mattered. She saw determination in the officer's eyes and wondered at the distance from the motorway to the nearest safety. Broken buildings loomed alongside them, an industrial estate. There was nothing there for her. Yes, motorway. That was what she had walked. She had dreamed of a Somewhere ahead, a place which held the lime-trees in flower, but she had come too far from the true green places. Not paid attention.

She went with him, into his black-white vehicle. Curious, not alarmed.

It wasn't far. Red lights and blue, the scurry of importance on people's faces as they passed. They herded her further from her roots and into the desolation of a place where the air was lifeless, warm without warmth. Hospital.

"You must see a doctor," one said, and so here she was.

The doctor, stiff white body in a stiff white coat, feels gently at her wrist, her neck. She allows this at first but does not know what he wants. Her throat starts to close tighter with every corridor they guide her down. He leads her to a bed by a window, where a woman makes her lie down. Nurse. That is another word. To nurture...

She looks around. A stunted cherry tree stands outside the building. A failed maypole in bloom. She clings to its presence and tries to ignore the worn shells which wheeze around it, drawing on their cigarettes and coughing like crows.

"You've been very lucky, miss. Miraculously so." The man shakes his head. "A few minor abrasions from a head-on collision? That's what they told me, anyway. Must have rolled with the impact somehow. Let's have a better look."

This is when Jump-Nancy comes to her again, head tilted wrong, arms all bent. Nancy is in the shadows, behind the things that wink and beep.

If they unclothe you, they'll see that you are hollow, Jump-Nancy whispers. *They will know you as huldre, inside as out.*

She hadn't thought. Already they are reaching to move her onto her side.

"No."

Their hands grow more insistent. She becomes alder, slick from the marshes, but they are reaching for pointed sticks, sharp metal needles, and it must stop. If they see, if they know she is hollow and hidden, it will be bad.

She lashes out, slamming the nurse into a cabinet, and one horn-soled foot catches the doctor between the legs, hard. He falls to his knees, moaning.

Up she comes, up through the open window and to the cherry tree, scrambling but not yet running. The wheezing ones move, a slow scatter of drip-stands and dressing-gowns, but it is a trap – the courtyard is enclosed. She and the tree are captives in a garden walled by hospital, with a policeman and a porter at the only doorway. Cigarette ends and blossoms swirl around her bare feet.

They take hold of her before she can appeal to the green places.

"Is she ill?" gasps the policeman, pinning her arms.

The doctor limps down the corridor, pauses.

"Maybe in the head." His thighs are tight together, protective. "Physically she's... strong as an ox. Fine. No obvious concussion, maybe a bit of bruising – not that she'll let me check the rest of her."

"Restraints?"

"We're not equipped. This is just a temporary assessment ward. I'll have to give her an injection while you hang on to her..."

She remembers the iron point. Hypodermic. No iron inside her. Ever.

Willow comes to her, cool as it weeps into the long waters, and she twists from the man's grip. She bends her slenderness round the doctor and the dazed nurse, sees real light beyond them down the corridor. Thirty paces, and there is real air as well. A metal box honks at her, but she remembers its kind now and slides round it.

Ambulance - she can read the strange words. And cars, lorries, vans, all manner of horrids.

But there are people, uniforms in her way...

She is in a low place of rooms and cells. It is a hive of square places, like wasps gone mad. Concrete and plastic. There is nothing for her to become as they push her into one of these rooms, empty and cold with the white glare of nothing on every wall.

"You need to tell us your name, miss," says a woman who is also police. "We want to help you."

"Huldre."

The officer shakes her head and takes a folder from the table in the middle of the room. Another man is watching, ready if she does anything.

"Look, love, we think that you're one of the patients who went missing from the Lowfields Unit, either Jennifer Davies or Nancy Wrightson. Do those names mean anything to you?"

Names again. There had been two women, two young women, once, far from here. And a meeting. Under the elm trees, when no-one was watching. Mutter-time.

We can leave. There's no-one on the gates.

That had been Jump-Nancy beneath the elms, picking at the beds of her fingernails. She had talked of freedoms, of many paths...

In this bright place, her captors watch.

"Do you know your name? Are you Jennifer, maybe, or Nancy?" The man speaks slowly, as to a child. She is not a child.

"Huldre."

"So you're not Jennifer or Nancy? Those names don't ring any bells?"

Speak not and keep the Within. Jump-Nancy is imperious, hiding beyond the corners.

The policewoman sighs. "There's a doctor coming, a special doctor to help you." She turns to her colleague. "There's been no sign of either of them for three days. Two blondes, similar enough. Early twenties, and both were supposedly on medication. They won't have any ID on them. Did a runner together in the night."

"Photographs on file?" He looks annoyed. "Fingerprints? Distinguishing marks?"

"They don't have a record. Nancy Wrightson was in for her own safety. Suicide risk. The other one, Jennifer, was just mad."

"Mad?" The man almost laughs. "That doesn't help a lot."

"I'm not a bloody psychiatrist. On the phone they said she talked about trees all the time. Someone's sending the details."

"She must be one of them, surely?" He frowns, as if he could identify her by staring hard enough.

"You'd think so. Don't know where she got those clothes, though."

"Charity shop? There's always stuff in the bin bags left outside the shops."

"Maybe."

This place is bad. She licks her lips.

"Water."

"I'll be OK with her," says the man.

The policewoman leaves the room.

"We're trying to help, you know." He scratches his neck, easing a tight shirt collar.

"Let free."

A shake of his head. "There's a procedure. You've no ID, you're wandering around barefoot and half-dressed - and you've been in a reported car accident. Add to that the fact that you assaulted a doctor..."

"No iron. Not in me."

He scratches again.

And she sees, through half-closed eyes, the way through, out. The door-frame and the boards which mark floor from wall. Not green, but the remembering of it. The tall pines ripped into corpse-wood and drained of their resinous lives. This was how gods were sacrificed, pierced in the side and nailed up for a world's sorrow.

The police woman returns, a notebook in her hands.

"Nancy Wrightson's dead. Topped herself, they think." She looks awkward, perhaps regretting her bluntness. "Uh, there was an incident by the rail line, out by Riggerton. Young woman seems to have thrown herself off the bridge. Positive ID on the body, from a Lowfields care assistant."

Jump-Nancy keep me, if you watch,
And if you're gone, then come once more.

They don't understand. She ignores their chatter and calls the pines, willing them into her.

"We think you're Jennifer Davies, love," says the man. "Does that ring any bells? Can you remember?"

He is trying to be kind. She can remember Nancy, remember Jennifer. She watched them, gathered between the elms, sharing their books and stolen chocolate bars, burying handfuls of tablets in the soft earth, scuffing the leaves over the grave. Small birds that would leave their cage.

Choices.

The memory of firs bends and sways, acknowledging her. Each knot in the boards weeps for her as she stands up.

"Huldre must leave."

They have not been bad, not forced things into her, so she will not punish them. The woman she pushes aside, the man she hits only hard enough to evade him. They cannot speak to the green places and are unknowing. Sturdy pine lets her force her way from the room, towards the outside; the faint memory of willow slips her between grasping hands.

Again, she is running.

She feels the chase, and knows that they will come, the angry red faces she has left behind, as she heads back into their warrens of made things. For one mayfly moment she scents the lime trees, and almost has hope. It is a direction, at least, in a world without any other.

The day is waning when she enters more of their destruction. Places which grind life and stink the air. Factories. She sees islands of mock-homes between them, rows of houses each with a dusty patch of grass, a few tame trees. And a gathering place, where people drink and laugh brittle-like, draining down the sun in gulps of false fruit and ferment. Alcohol.

Her feet patter on gravel, concrete, and she hugs to a fence so that she can watch. Jump-Nancy knows these people. Or their type.

This is the ritual, breaking barriers with the drink, making plans of semen and diesel. They press close, sometimes to be thrust away. Laughter, scorn and suggestion. *Not tonight. Maybe next time. He'll be waiting for me. She doesn't know about us. They'll still be awake.*

Part of her would be there among them, to feel flesh rather than concrete. Touching. Not her kind, though, and they would soon know her for what she was. She turns, but there are figures on the street behind her. They stare.

"Jesus, she looks a bit gone," says a large woman. "What is that she's wearing?"

"It's the distressed hippy look," says another. "I read about it."

"That's not distressed, it's bloody derelict."

Huldre drifts long fingers down her body, the soft dress of dandelion seeds and thistledown she thinks she has always worn, memories of the green places, dyed only with nettle, with madder and urine. Her sisters made it for her in the wildwood, even as they told her that the hollow should never go to the metal places. Even as she failed to listen.

"Mine," she says, not accepting shame.

"Oh my God!" The third woman, scrawny and hare-faced, shrieks. "It's the girl they're looking for, that one who attacked some cops. The mental case. I saw the newsfeed."

They huddle back, hard to the fence. One pulls a small cylinder from her bag, holds it up as if she were using a cross to ward off evil.

"Keep away. Cindy, phone the cops."

The hare-faced woman stabs thin fingers at something in her hand, a plastic thing that beeps like the hospital room.

She does not think that she likes these people. There is yellowed grass and ivy around her feet, the ivy smoke-sick or poisoned, blackened. She is tempted to hurt them, to take on tendrils, thick strangling stems, and punish them, though she does not. That is their pollution as well, the urge to hurt. She can feel it growing inside her, a poisoned seed.

She twists and is away, dancing the green places as best she can, from the sad ivy to a patch of lawn, a bush which someone has tended – anywhere. Garden to cramped garden, away from the shrieking women. The lakes of her past are ponds filled with captives. Fish which will never swim far or free; water-plants whose roots hit plastic liners, not the deep oozing mud of life.

A small boy calls out, not in wonder but in derision.

She is hurting.

Sirens roam the last light of the day. Some are for her, she knows. A police car drives her deeper into a maze of dead streets, and she grows tired, too tired. There are more gardens, but they are small and mean, with little on which to draw.

She runs jagged, slapping a hand against each roadside tree to find what comfort she can. A sycamore lends her life, reminds her what she is, and at last she catches the scent of blossom properly, not so very far away.

Not so very far away. The thought reverberates, revitalizes. Two, three of the shrieking metal boxes are closing on her; a high wall of plywood sheets and corrugated iron blocks her path. Despite this, she is excited. There is a green place greater than any she has found here, in the midst of their wasteland.

Jump-Nancy speaks to her. *It is their conscience, a reminder of what they should be. A park, a place of healing. A Growing, by those who diminish all else.*

She can see what lies behind the wall, behind fluttering posters for events long gone. A half-constructed – or half-ruined - mass of glass and concrete stands between her and the pool of green.

A deep, unfettered breath. She smells lime-flowers again, and hears the small makers in their thousands, their mottled coats brushed with the powder that brings forth wonders. Miner and cutter and bumble and more, returning as the sun sets. Why this thing is here, so ugly next to beauty, she cannot comprehend.

The men and women in uniform have left their vehicles, and are closing on her – some wary, some singing songs of false hope. The wall is hard, but the sycamore's blessing helps her over. Beyond is digging and making, the brutal holes, the empty pipes in disarray. Building site? Another set of their words vaguely recalled. Tiring, she fails to notice the crouched figure until it speaks, a rasp of breath.

"They're always after you f'something."

The old woman squats in half-darkness, a bundle of worn coats and scarves.

Huldre pauses.

"I am not bad. Inside, outside."

"Shouldn't think y'are. I like your dress."

"Thank? Thank you." That seems the right thing to say.

The woman tilts her head at the sounds of the sirens. She has the face of yew trees, dark and peeling. Hard eyes, but with a glint of sweeter memories.

"What'll y'do now, girlie?"

Her pursuers will find a way round, or over, the outside walls, and she must choose, high or low. To bury herself in the tainted soil around her and wait, hope that they grow bored. Or to fly like Jump-Nancy. The choice is natural, instinctive. There are only the heights to seek.

"I will fly."

The old woman nods. "Good f'you."

Huldre climbs steadily, first on metal tubes and platforms, then up walls of raw brick and concrete. Her grip is good, fingers and toes, for she is ivy and mistletoe, born to cling and taste the air.

Shouts from below; alarm at her actions.

"Come down, love. It's all right!"

They are unknowing.

High on the crude scaffolding, she sees the world that is not hers, a glinting, over-lit unmaking of soft hills and deep, cold rivers. A death of grass, an attempt to manage the things they fear. In a sudden shiver, she is not without sympathy.

We must all choose, eventually, says Jump-Nancy. *You know that I did.*

The breeze is free of human voices, free of disgust or entreaty. And there, below her, on the far side of this constructed thing, the lime trees are waiting for night – and for her. She sees Nancy, sees Jennifer, as they plotted their escape, and she knows what they wanted. What they chose.

Spreading her arms wide, the wind catches at her hollow back and welcomes the truths within her. As she launches herself into the air, she smiles. She has become thistledown, to be borne down towards the green places. There will be freedom, of many kinds.

Jump-Nancy keep me, if you watch.

For she is falling…

CONTRIBUTORS

Aeron Alfrey creates unique imagery inspired by the fantastic, grotesque and monstrous. His art has been published in numerous books and shown in galleries around the world.

s. j. bagley is a multidisciplinary artist, philosopher, and critic what lives in the woods near the ocean. they edit and publish *Thinking Horror: A Journal of Horror Philosophy*, and their long running sound art tribute to arthropods, *keziah mason*, has just entered its fifteenth year. the regular host of the arcade asylum reading series at the lovecraft arts & sciences council, much of their work can be found at heksenhaus.tumblr.com, and they generally wish you well.

F. J. Bergmann edits poetry for *Mobius: The Journal of Social Change* (mobiusmagazine.com) and imagines tragedies on or near exoplanets. She has competed at National Poetry Slam as a member of the Madison, WI, Urban Spoken Word team. Her work appears irregularly in *Abyss & Apex, Analog, Asimov's SF,* and elsewhere in the alphabet. *A Catalogue of the Further Suns* won the 2017 Gold Line Press poetry chapbook contest and the 2018 SFPA Elgin Chapbook Award.

Emmie Bristow grew up in Helena, Montana. She has had work featured in Z Publishing's *An Anthology of Emerging Poets*, Dramatic Pen Press's *Into the Beautiful: Poetry by Montana Artists Volumes I, II, and III*, as well as university publications such as the editor's edition of the University of Montana's *The Oval* and Carroll

College's *Colors*. She currently holds a BA in English (emphasis on creative writing and literature) from the University of Montana and is working toward her MFA in poetry at Drew University. She currently lives in Missoula, Montana.

Michael Cisco is an American writer, Deleuzian academic, teacher, and translator currently living in New York City. He is best known for his first novel, *The Divinity Student*, winner of the International Horror Guild Award for Best First Novel of 1999. His novel, *The Great Lover*, was nominated for the 2011 Shirley Jackson Award for Best Novel of the Year and declared the Best Weird Novel of 2011 by the *Weird Fiction Review*.

S. L. Edwards is a Texan currently living in California. He loves it, stereotypes be damned. He enjoys dark fiction, poetry and darker beer. His debut collection of short stories, *Whiskey and Other Unusual Ghosts,* is forthcoming from Gehenna and Hinnom Books in 2019.

Kurt Fawver is a Shirley Jackson Award-winning writer of horror, weird fiction, and literature that oozes through the cracks of genre. His short fiction has previously appeared in venues such as *The Magazine of Fantasy & Science Fiction, Strange Aeons, Weird Tales, Vastarien,* and *Gamut* and has been chosen for inclusion in *Best New Horror* and *Year's Best Weird Fiction*. He's also released two collections of short stories, *The Dissolution of Small Worlds* and *Forever, in Pieces* as well as one novella, *Burning Witches, Burning Angels*. Kurt has also had non-fiction published in journals such as *Thinking Horror* and the *Journal of the Fantastic in the Arts*. He hopes you enjoy the fruits of his bizarre labors.

John Linwood Grant is a professional writer/editor who lives in Yorkshire with a pack of lurchers and a beard. He has had many contemporary weird and dark period fictions published in magazines and anthologies over the last few years, including the *Tales of the Last Edwardian* series - murder, madness and the supernatural. He enjoys subverting the classic themes of weird fiction, his favorite word is ab-natural, and his most popular character is Mr. Bubbles, a bad-tempered, slightly psychotic pony who regularly put an ironic, iron-shod hoof through cosmic horror. His latest novel, *The Assassin's Coin* concerns spiritualism, the lethal Mr. Dry and a fresh take on the Autumn of Terror in Whitechapel. He edits the magazine *Occult Detective Quarterly* and is currently putting together the anthology *Hell's Empire*, featuring an Incursion of daemonic forces into late Victorian Britain. His eclectic website greydogtales.com explores weird fiction and weird art. And lurchers.

Michael Hutter is a German artist born in 1963, whose surreal works are as magical as they are strange. Since 1986 he has been exhibiting his work in numerous art galleries.

S. T. Joshi is a freelance writer and editor. He has prepared comprehensive editions of Lovecraft's collected fiction, essays, and poetry. He is the author of *The Weird Tale* (1990), *The Modern Weird Tale* (2001), *I Am Providence: The Life and Times of H. P. Lovecraft* (2010), and *Unutterable Horror: A History of Supernatural Fiction* (2012), and has edited the anthology *American Supernatural Tales* (2007).

Tonya Liburd shares a birthday with Simeon Daniel and Ray Bradbury, which may tell you a little something about her. Hailed by Rich Horton as one of ten persons worthy of getting the Campbell Award for Best New Writer, she has been nominated for the 2017 and 2018 Rhysling Awards and has been longlisted in the 2015 Carter V. Cooper/Exile Short Fiction Competition. Nisi Shawl and Tananarive Due both use her work in their workshops and courses. She is also the Senior Editor of *Abyss & Apex Magazine*. You can find her blogging at http://Spiderlilly.com or on Twitter at @somesillywowzer.

L'Erin Ogle is an author living in Lawrence, KS. She has stories published at *Syntax & Salt*, *Metaphorosis*, and *Trampset*, with upcoming work at *Daily Science Fiction*. She can be found online at lerinogle@gmail.com.

Sam Schreiber's work has appeared in Martian Migraine Press, *Analog Science Fiction, Fact, Tales to Terrify* and *Occult Detective Quarterly*. He teaches Science Fiction and Fantasy at NYU Tandon and lives in Brooklyn with his wife and the neighbor cat who drops by sometimes.

Sean M. Thompson is from Massachusetts. He loves horror and anything weird. He is the author of the chapbook *Too Late*, the novel *TH3 D3MON*, the bizarro novella *Hate From The Sky*, has a story in the chapbook *Letters of Decline*, and is the author of the novella *Farmington Correctional*. His work has appeared in the anthologies *Test Patterns*, and *Terror in 16-bits*. He is also the co-host of the comedic horror/ weird podcast *Miskatonic Musings*. You can find him on twitter @spookyseanT or at his official website seanmthompsonfiction.com.

Dr. Raymond Thoss is a Licensed Psychologist and has spent his career working primarily with child trauma victims. He has worked, and is currently working, at both the state and national level on child trauma initiatives. He is currently faculty at a Tier 1 University where he serves child abuse victims and their families. He teaches, conducts research, trains providers, and provides direct care as part of his current position.

Toni Tošić, a Serbian artist, is influenced by natural decay, accidents, serendipity, and the god(s).

Yves Tourigny is a bipedal animal frequently mistaken for a small bear or well-fed raccoon. The product of billions of years of evolutionary pressure and sexual selection, his accomplishments fit comfortably on an index card.

Michael Uhall is a political theorist and an aficionado of horrific and weird prose. He is currently finishing his Ph.D. in political science, and he is also writing two novels. One is about a revolution on a cruise ship, and the other is a psychogeographical horror story about the bleakness at the heart of the American historical experience.

Brooke Warra grew up in a deep, dark wood where she developed a taste for the weird and macabre. Her work has appeared in various magazines, anthologies, and podcasts. She lives and writes with her children in the Pacific Northwest.

Rayna Waxhead is a writer and amateur sacred clown who lives in Los Angeles with her wife and two cats. She strives to create work that is simultaneously playful, strange, beautiful, and horrific. She is a member of the Horror Writers Association and also writes under her alter ego Kendra Temples. You can find her online at raynawaxhead.com.

A Pushcart Prize nominee and award-winning short story writer, **Désirée Zamorano's** stories and essays have appeared online an in print including in *The Los Angeles Times, Huizache Magazine* and *Kenyon Review*. Her highly acclaimed literary novel *The Amado Women* is about four Latinas linked by birth, separated by secrets.